AMERICAN TOPICS

Jorge Olan Morales

AMERICAN TOPICS

*A Reading-Vocabulary Text
for Speakers of English
as a Second Language*

SECOND EDITION

Robert C. Lugton

PRENTICE HALL REGENTS
Englewood Cliffs, New Jersey 07632

Library of Congress Cataloging-in-Publication Data
Main entry under title:

American topics.

    1. English language—Text-books for foreign speakers.
2. Readers—United States. 3. Vocabulary. I. Lugton,
Robert C.
PE1128.A478 1986   428.2'4   85–16732
ISBN 0–13–029588–4

Editorial/production supervision and
   interior design: Debbie Ford
Cover design: Joe Curcio
Manufacturing buyer: Harry P. Baisley

Acknowledgments appear on page 261 which constitutes
a continuation of the copyright page.

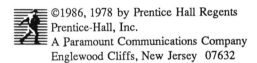©1986, 1978 by Prentice Hall Regents
Prentice-Hall, Inc.
A Paramount Communications Company
Englewood Cliffs, New Jersey 07632

Printed in the United States of America

20 19 18 17 16 15

ISBN   0-13-029588-4

Prentice-Hall International (UK) Limited, *London*
Prentice-Hall of Australia Pty. Limited, *Sydney*
Prentice-Hall Canada Inc., *Toronto*
Prentice-Hall Hispanoamericana, S.A., *Mexico*
Prentice-Hall of India Private Limited, *New Delhi*
Prentice-Hall of Japan, Inc., *Tokyo*
Simon & Schuster Asia Pte. Ltd., *Singapore*
Editora Prentice-Hall do Brasil, Ltda., *Rio de Janeiro*

This book is dedicated to Borinquen Lugton, a constant source of help and advice.

AMERICAN TOPICS

CONTENTS

PREFACE

The original edition of *American Topics* was favorably received. To diversify the readings of the earlier version and provide additional language learning activities is the purpose of the second edition.

As before, this text is intended for students of English as a second language at or above the intermediate level. Each of the fifteen chapters centers on some aspect of American life. Some present opinion; some provide factual perspective. All have been planned around contemporary issues of concern to older adolescents and adult students, and all have been especially written or adapted for this volume.

Language learning can be fun—it has the obligation to be interesting. With this in mind, the essays in this book were picked for provocative reading. Because today's students care about their world, some essays are concerned with controversial issues, the kind discussed each day in the press and popular magazines. These topics range from marriage to pollution, from ecology to wildlife management. But there are also themes in a lighter vein—popular music, food, and sports. To these the second edition adds chapters on choosing a career, women's liberation, a visit to the Grand Canyon. The chapters are all informative; some raise social consciousness. This is a book that can be used by students in schools overseas as well as in America.

To stimulate interest and motivate discussion, each chapter presents pictures, a map, or other visuals, and concludes with a set of language exercises that cover the following: questions for oral response, vocabulary, synonyms and antonyms, word-form practice, prepositions and other structure words, idioms and special expressions, reading comprehension, composition topics, dictation. The new edition includes skits, language games, controlled compositions, and hand-writing improvement. The text provides ample material for a reading-vocabu-lary class that meets from three to five hours a week for fifteen weeks. A class with fewer weekly meetings can, of course, also use this text.

The aim of this book is the development in students of an active, not passive, command of English. The additions in readings and exercises in the second edition should assist students to reach this goal.

Robert C. Lugton

INTRODUCTION

Guidelines for the Teacher

These materials are designed for the intermediate level, a transition phase in language learning when the student moves from the rigidly-controlled work of the beginners' class, with its restrictions on syntax and vocabulary, toward a less-structured approach, in which the ability to ask questions, participate in discussions, read unadapted material, and write with comparative ease is assumed. This is a critical stage in language learning, when the student must evolve from a halting speaker to a fluent conversationalist, with reading, writing, and comprehension skills to match—a crucial transformation.

Progress at this stage can be greatly facilitated if the presentation of materials is keyed by the teacher to the language capability of his or her students, this capability being quite variable, as we have seen, at the intermediate level. With a less proficient group, a more controlled approach is desired. As proficiency improves, controls can be gradually relaxed; exercises that can progressively increase the degree of challenge and difficulty are needed at this level. *American Topics* provides this flexibility. For teachers unfamiliar with the technique, the following suggestions are provided as general guidelines to the use of the readings and exercises in this text.

Reading

Apart from an occasional passage of unusual complexity, there is no reason to have a selection read aloud in class.* In fact, that is a misuse of class time. Reading is a silent, receptive activity—the process of getting meaning from the printed word. It is better to have the students prepare each story as an out-of-class assignment. This develops good reading habits, too, for in resolving comprehension difficulties on their own, students acquire self-reliance. And they more rapidly transfer to English the reading skill they possess in their first language, that of reading directly for meaning. They should mark difficult concepts and structures in the margin of the text for questions in class later on (if these are not anticipated by the teacher when the reading is introduced). Any residual difficulties in comprehension will clear up when the students do the oral and written exercises at the end of the chapter.

Some techniques do make reading easier. To begin with, students should read the selection several times to grasp the meaning as a whole, without pausing to look up every unfamiliar word in the dictionary. Looking up words at this point will simply obscure the overall picture and immerse the student in a mass of disconnected detail.

Secondly, the meaning of many words can be guessed if the reader uses a general knowledge of the subject and fits together related information from the surrounding text. A phrase here, a sentence there, define, restate, summarize, add details, or in some way clarify the passage. Such context clues, deliberately inserted by the writer to make the meaning clear, abound in these selections. Students should be taught to find and understand them. For instance:

A. Do you like *coq au vin,* a chicken-and-wine dish from France?

B. The pioneer family had already traveled a long distance. They and all their belongings were packed in a *covered wagon,* which was horse drawn and could only travel six miles a day.

One need not be an expert on French cooking to understand *coq au vin,* so explicitly is it defined in Example A. In Example B, the references to *travel, horse*

---

*The exceptions to this rule are the chapter prefaces, which are to be read in class as part of the Preview activity.

drawn, and *six miles a day* clearly mark *covered wagon* as a slow-moving vehicle of some kind. There is no need for students to skip past unfamiliar expressions. Enough can be inferred about these words from the context for the reader to move on with an acceptable degree of comprehension. Application of this technique should be encouraged by the teacher, using examples from each reading assignment, until the students can apply the method automatically.

Context clues, though helpful, cannot clarify every word. For a precise definition, the student must use a dictionary, but, it is hoped, not a bilingual edition. That practice should be discouraged. Looking for a native-language equivalent for every English word (and writing it interlinearly in the text) inhibits bilingualism, retards vocabulary building, and makes the student first-language-dependent for a long time. On the other hand, the monolingual English dictionary (any of the many pocket-size versions will do) provides not only a definition but synonyms, antonyms, and other useful information. But be sure the students understand how to use the dictionary, how to look up words and interpret the abbreviations in the entry. A unit is provided in the appendix for dictionary practice. Many teachers find a review of this section helpful at the beginning of the semester.

Lesson Plan

Organize the treatment of each chapter into three broad divisions—*Preview, Practice,* and *Review*—to be spread over the total time available in the week for that chapter. The *Preview* is the introductory phase, when the new selection is scanned for vocabulary and structure. Have the students look through the reading in class, paying particular attention to the pictures and the preview paragraphs that preface each chapter. Your purpose at this stage is to familiarize the students with the subject matter and motivate them to do the reading assignment. In the *Practice* sessions, which should be spread over several class periods, go through the reading assignments to check for comprehension, and do the oral drills and exercises. The *Review* is the final phase. This should not be a mere repetition of exercises already done, but something new, at a higher level of difficulty. It should resemble "real" language activities as much as possible.

Remember that pace and variety are important. Practice all the language skills by including different types of activities in each lesson. Intersperse controlled drills with free discussion, seatwork with boardwork, students working singly with students in groups.

The following weekly plan provides variety.

Weekly Lesson Plan

I
PREVIEW
First Day

1. Question-and-answer drill using the pictures.	5–10 minutes
2. Discussion or question-and-answer drill using the chapter preface.	5 minutes

II
PRACTICE
Several Days

1. Scanning Exercise (Include line-by-line questions of this type on the initial and each succeeding day until the chapter has been covered.)	15 minutes
2. Reading Comprehension	5–10 minutes
3. Vocabulary Development	10 minutes
4. Vocabulary	
5. Synonyms	
6. Word-form Chart	
7. Word-form Practice	30–40 minutes
8. Prepositions	
9. Idioms	

III
REVIEW
Final Day

1. Special Activity Skit, debate, discussion, game	30–40 minutes
2. Dictation	5–10 minutes
3. Quiz	10 minutes

Preview: Using the Pictures

The pictures provide a great deal of information at a glance. They not only keynote the story line but also illustrate vocabulary. Use them as the focal point for questions. Since you will want to practice structure as well as vocabulary, many variations are possible. But the Preview lesson, whatever its focus, should be carefully planned beforehand, with a specific structure and set of lexical items in mind.

Ask for the name, function, location, number, size, color, use, value, purpose, or whatever else is illustrated in the picture, writing the new words on the blackboard. Have the students copy the words, brief definitions, synonyms, and the like in their notebooks.

This question practice can be conducted at several levels of difficulty, depending on the proficiency of the class. For example:

METHOD 1

Referring to the picture, the teacher asks a question, introducing a vocabulary item.

How many *baskets of shrimp* do you see?

Student

I see three *baskets of shrimp.*

The practice continues with the teacher asking similar questions about other objects in the picture.

METHOD 2

Referring to the picture, the teacher gives the vocabulary item and the question word.

baskets of shrimp/how many

Student A (composes the question).

How many *baskets of shrimp* do you see?

Student B (responds).

I see three *baskets of shrimp.*

METHOD 3 (ADVANCED)

A. The teacher puts a short list of words relating to the picture on the board. Using these words, students take turns composing questions and calling on other students to answer. In this method, the teacher remains largely silent, monitoring the exchange and supplying help when it is requested.

B. In another variation, the students write out the questions and exchange papers with a neighbor who writes the answers. Papers are returned to the owners for correction.

C. In still another variation, as follow-up to any of the above or as a quiz later on, the students, using the words on the board with books open to the picture, write questions. To continue the practice in structure and vocabulary, they can answer their own questions or exchange with another student. The papers are corrected and graded by the teacher. If desired, this exercise can be structured by restricting grammar and vocabulary in some way: to count questions using "how many?" to ownership questions using "whose?" to location questions using "where?" and so on.

Preview: Using the Chapter Prefaces

Each reading is preceded by a paragraph or two of background information. After the picture practice, the preface can be read in class and used in various ways to lay additional foundation. For instance, Chapter One is about two students visiting the Grand Canyon. The preface presents some facts on our national parks system. Since most countries have set aside wilderness areas like ours, students are familiar with the concept, and can name a comparable reserve in their own country. Turn this into a vocabulary-building, question-response practice, using key words from the preface, such as "hike," "camp," "watch birds." For maximum effect, answers should be complete sentences, not one-word responses.

Teacher – Question	Student – Answer
Does your country have any parks?	Yes, my country has many parks.
Are the parks large or small?	The parks are very large.
Can you hike there?	Yes, you can hike there.
Can you camp there?	Yes, you can camp there, too.

All these activities suggest outdoor recreation. But the national parks have a serious side, too. So, for more proficient classes, questions about using the parks to conserve natural resources, preserve plants and wildlife, and advance education would be appropriate. Each of the chapter prefaces lends itself to treatment of this kind to motivate the reading assignment.

Practice

At the next class, do the Scanning Exercise. It takes the student through the text line by line. The questions should not be answered with a response read directly from the book. A better technique is as follows: The teacher asks the question (or gives a cue). All the students glance at their books, formulate the response, and then look at the teacher, eyes off the text. A student is called on to give the answer.

As with the picture practice, this exercise can also be done in several ways. Begin with Method 1, then move to Methods 2 and 3 as the class becomes more proficient.

METHOD 1

Teacher reads a question from the Scanning Exercise Response.	How long is the Grand Canyon?
Student glances at appropriate page in text for information, then looks up and responds.	The Grand Canyon is 277 miles long.

METHOD 2

Teacher reads a line directly from the text and gives a question word.	The students visited the Grand Canyon? Who?
Student A (composes the question)	Who visited the Grand Canyon?
Student B	The students visited the Grand Canyon.

The teacher might continue the drill by repeating the same line with a different question word (such as *what*), or by going on to the next line in the text.

METHOD 3 (**ADVANCED**)

Student A reads a line from the text.	Jazz belongs to the people.
Student B composes a question.	What belongs to the people?
Student C answers the question.	Jazz belongs to the people.
Student D creates a new question from the original line.	Whom does jazz belong to?
Student E responds.	Jazz belongs to the people.

The Other Exercises

The synonym, vocabulary, word-form, and verb exercises, which require prior study, should be written first. Then they can be done as oral drills. A word of caution. Before assigning the fill-in exercises that use word lists, tell the students to keep their options open. A word from the list may appear to fill the blank only to be needed for a sentence later on. Some shifting around of words is to be expected.

Games

Language games are a pleasant way to practice vocabulary and structure. They provide a change of pace and allow for socialization and impromptu communication, while competition improves class morale and motivates learning.

In the text, some of the games are included in the lessons; others are grouped in the appendix. The latter can be adapted by the teacher to fit most of the readings. So, to enliven the regular mix of learning activities, include a game or two each week.

Controlled Compositions

Each chapter contains a controlled composition. This is structured practice in which the student rewrites a model passage, changing syntax or vocabulary according to the directions at the bottom of the page. These changes can involve the number or person of the noun, the verb tense, vocabulary, or some other variable. Such revisions, once begun, echo through the paragraph, and the student must continue to restructure until the passage is consistent again.

Each composition provides two steps to allow teaching flexibility. Students who need extra practice can do both; advanced students can be assigned the more difficult step, and so forth.

This is the time and place to impart good writing habits. Teachers do their students no favor by accepting careless work. Punctuation, paragraphing, headings, indention, and all other conventions of arranging words on paper should be stressed. Students with handwriting problems can be referred to the penmanship section in the appendix, which may prove particularly useful to those whose native alphabet is not Roman.

Review

In the *Review,* the students should have a chance to put into practice what they have learned. Turn each of the stories into a skit or role play of some kind, with students extemporizing on their version of the topic—ordering a meal in a restaurant, counseling a married couple, planning a vacation. A debate, with the class taking sides on a controversial issue, is excellent practice.

Composition

The final measure of language learning is the students' use of vocabulary in meaningful communications of their own. The composition topics are designed to tie together the students' interests and experience with what they have studied in the reading. Have students use the new vocabulary in writing of their own. Sometimes a list of key words is provided by the teacher.

Dictation

A dictation is provided at the end of each chapter to follow the oral practice and written homework. It tests aural comprehension and the ability to write correctly what is said. It also tests retention, spelling, and syntax.

Sentences for dictation should be practiced in one class and given at the next. The teacher should speak in a normal voice, should not read slowly, word by word, and should not repeat the sentence more than three or four times. Feel free to change some of the words to add an element of surprise.

Here are three variations on the straight dictation. The first is the dicto-comp. From the reading, the teacher selects a paragraph that contains about 100 words. Read this paragraph to the class several times. The students listen carefully. After the last reading, the students write the paragraph as they remember it, staying as close as possible to the original. They should not write while the teacher is reading, but must wait until the reading is finished and the paragraph understood. This exercise combines dictation with original composition since the student must create to fill in memory gaps.

In another variation, the teacher selects an incident from the story and presents it to the class in an abbreviated form. The students are asked to recreate the episode supplying all the missing details.

Still another variation uses the Scanning Questions. These will have been practiced ahead of time and are familiar to the class. The teacher asks the questions; the class writes the questions and the answer.

Follow-Through Activities

Reading skill is acquired by reading—extensive reading of all kinds. Intensive class exercises like these should be followed up by out-of-class reading of some kind. Novels, short stories, and plays are all readily available in paperback. A class play or a book report make suitable end-of-semester activities. Helping students make a long range plan for outside reading would be, perhaps, the most appropriate way to conclude this course.

One

THE GRAND CANYON

A Wonderful Place to Visit

Last year, about 6.5 million people visited the United States from overseas. Most visitors entered the country through one of the large cities—New York, Boston, Miami, Los Angeles, San Francisco. Then, having landed in a city, the newcomers simply "stayed put,"[1] not realizing that the interior of the country offered travel opportunities of unusual beauty and interest. Did you know that between Maine and California there are 41 national parks? Some parks cover thousands of acres. Each has its own distinctive scenery and character. If you like nature study, hiking, camping, bird-watching, clean air, quiet, or just getting away from the city, you will love the national parks. On the East Coast, for example, there is Acadia National Park, Maine.[2] It faces the Atlantic Ocean and has a long, rocky coastline. On the West Coast, in California, there are Yosemite, with majestic mountains, forests, and rivers; and Death Valley, with desert plants and animals. In between are enough national and state parks to satisfy every taste and interest: Cape Hatteras, North Carolina; Great Smoky Mountains, Tennessee; Shenandoah, Virginia. Above all, there is the Grand Canyon, Arizona, that mighty chasm carved in the earth by the Colorado River. Visiting a national park need not be expensive for the overseas visitor, but it does require advance information and careful planning.

[1]"stayed put"—didn't move around and see the country.
[2]To locate the states mentioned in this paragraph, refer to the map on p. 178.

1

VISITING THE GRAND CANYON

vista

(1) The Grand Canyon is an impressive sight. It is 277 miles long, between 4 and 18 miles wide, and more than a mile deep. No one knows for sure how the canyon was made, but geologists generally agree that over millions of years, the Colorado River, which runs down the center of the canyon, gradually cut through the sand and rock to carve this mighty chasm. This wearing-down process is called erosion. The wind and natural land movements did the rest. Today, the Grand Canyon is a geologist's dream. The rock layers in the sides of the canyon are exposed to view. Each layer is a record of all the natural events that happened to the land through eons of time. In one layer, there is dust from an ancient volcano. In another layer, there is sand from a lake that once covered the area. In a third layer, there are the bones of prehistoric animals. The canyon is like a storybook. If you had enough knowledge, you could unravel the history of the earth.

(2) But studying geology is not the only interesting thing to do there. It is an ideal place to hike, to ride a bike, to take a boat ride down the river, to camp out overnight, to take photographs, and to see beautiful scenery. To add further

Notice the different levels of rock and earth in the walls of the canyon—like layers in a cake.

dust - polvo   deep - hondo .   chasm .   layers = capas
bones = hues os   sand - arena   wearing - down .   eons = miles

interest, the canyon has six different climate zones, and many kinds of plants, trees, and animals.

(*3*)   "We've got to see the Grand Canyon," said José to his friend Ibrahim. José is from Colombia, South America, and speaks Spanish. Ibrahim is from Egypt, and speaks Arabic. To communicate, they have to speak English.

(*4*)   "Let's go," said Ibrahim. "School doesn't start for three weeks. We'll just have time. I saved some money from my summer job, but how will we get there? We don't have a car."

(*5*)   "There are three ways," José said. "We could fly or go by train, but that would be expensive, so let's take the bus. It explains how in this booklet. There are two major interurban bus lines in the U.S.—Greyhound and Trailways," said José, reading from the booklet. "These two companies operate 6,700 buses and carry over 350,000,000 passengers each year—more than the railroads and the airlines combined. Best of all, bus travel is relatively cheap."

(*6*)   "This sounds like a great trip, and practical, too. When do we start?" asked Ibrahim.

(*7*)   "What about Monday? That would give us plenty of time to pack." *suficiente*

(*8*)   "Monday's okay with me," Ibrahim said. "I'm taking one suitcase, some casual clothes, and my hiking boots."

(*9*)   "Travel light. That's my motto," José said. "And carry traveler's checks. They're safer than cash."

(*10*)   Monday rolled around in no time. The two friends caught the bus at the depot. Next morning, they were in Flagstaff, Arizona, gateway city to the Grand Canyon. A local bus took them the rest of the way, about 80 miles, and dropped them at the Park entrance.

(*11*)   Now their excitement began to rise. They could hardly wait to view the canyon itself. But they were in for a surprise. At first there was nothing

Interurban bus travel is convenient and relatively cheap.

unravel = desenrollar

special to see. Dark green pine trees surrounded the boys on every side. They seemed to be in the middle of a forest. Fortunately, the trail to the canyon was well marked. "Grand Canyon this way," read a sign.

(*12*)   It took ten minutes of rapid walking to reach the canyon. The boys stumbled on it, really, for there was no preparation, no gradual slope, just flat, wooded country that suddenly disappeared into the mile-deep abyss.

(*13*)   "Wow," said José. "Look at that!"

(*14*)   "Wow," repeated Ibrahim, unable to find better words.

(*15*)   It was a thrilling sight. The rocky precipice at the top fell straight down to the canyon floor, which was very uneven and covered with rocks. Cutting down the middle was the wild Colorado River, although from this distance it looked like a harmless stream. The other side of the canyon was clearly visible. Overhead, a hawk flew lazily in a cloudless sky. The boys could see for a hundred miles in every direction.

(*16*)   "What'll we do first?" José asked.

(*17*)   Just at that moment, the boys noticed a park ranger standing beside a big picture of the canyon. "Right now, we're standing on the south rim, or edge,

The park ranger takes people on guided tours. The ranger explains rock formations and identifies local trees, flowers, and animals.

Dinosaurs were extinct millions of years ago.

of the canyon, just about here," the ranger said, indicating a place on the picture. "That's the north rim over there," he said, pointing across the canyon. "Did you notice how the rocks and earth are arranged like layers in a cake, and that each layer has a different color? The layer at the bottom of the canyon is the oldest. It is called Early Precambrian," the ranger said, giving the scientific name. "These rocks must be about 1.7 billion years old. The rocks on top are younger. Each layer has a different age, and has characteristic deposits that correspond to the geological and natural events occurring at the time. We find evidence of animal life at this level," said the ranger, pointing to a layer near the top. "Probably dinosaurs, extinct animals that lived millions of years ago."

(18)   "Isn't this interesting," said Ibrahim. "When I get back to school, I'm going to do some research in geology and write a paper for my science class."

research = estudio

Starved = hambriento
Supper = dinner

(19) "Yes, it is interesting," said José, "but I'm getting hungry. Isn't it time for supper?"

(20) There were several places to eat. The boys could get fast food at a lunch stand or dinner in the restaurant.

(21) "Let's go to the restaurant," said Ibrahim. "I'm starved."

(22) After a short wait, they were seated at a table. The waiter arrived to take their order.

(23) "I'm so hungry, I could eat a dinosaur," said José, glancing at the menu. "I'm going to have vegetable soup, steak, mashed potatoes, lettuce salad, and ice cream for dessert."

(24) Ibrahim ordered mushroom soup, veal stew with rice, tomato salad, and apple pie.

(25) When the boys had finished eating, they glanced out the window. The sun was just setting. If they hurried, they could just get outside in time to watch the sun drop below the canyon rim, which it did with a burst of many colors.

(26) "Wasn't this a great day?" José said. "What'll we do tomorrow?"

Exercises

1

SCANNING *This exercise follows the story line by line, from sentence 1. The teacher asks the questions. The students, books open, scan the page for information, then, looking up, give the response—in a complete sentence, eyes off the text.*

1. What is an impressive sight?
2. How long is the Grand Canyon?
3. How wide is the Grand Canyon?
4. How deep is the Grand Canyon?
5. Which river runs down the center of the Canyon?
6. What did the river cut through?
7. What is this process called?
8. Which natural forces did the rest?
9. Whose dream is the Grand Canyon today?
10. Which layers in the Canyon are exposed to view?
11. Where can you find a record of natural events?
12. What do you find in the first layer? *dust of ancient volcano*
13. What do you find in another layer? *Sand of the late*
14. What do you find in a third layer? *bones of prehistoric animals*

15. What is like a storybook?
16. With enough knowledge, what could you unravel? *history of earth*
17. What else can you do at the Canyon? (Repeat the question for the various activities.) *(calumet?)*
18. How many climate zones does the Canyon have? *6*
19. What country is José from?
20. What language does he speak?
21. What country is Ibrahim from?
22. What language does he speak?
23. How do they communicate?
24. How much time did they have before school?
25. How did they decide to travel?

2

VOCABULARY DEVELOPMENT   *Study the following words, numbered according to the paragraph where each word occurs in the story. Then do exercise 3.*

canyon (1)	**interurban** (5)
geologist (1)	**motto** (9)
million (1)	**traveler's checks** (9)
erosion (1)	**rim** (of the canyon) (17)
layer (1)	**dinosaur** (17)
volcano (1)	**fast food** (20)

lunch stand (20)

1. A **canyon** is a deep valley or crack in the earth, often with steep sides. *Chasm* (1) and *abyss* (12) are synonyms for **canyon.**
2. A **geologist** studies the history and structure of the earth by analyzing rocks and other natural earth features.
3. A **million** is one thousand thousands (1,000,000); a *billion* is one thousand millions (1,000,000,000).
4. **Erosion** is a process that changes the earth's surface through the action of natural forces like wind and water.
5. A **layer** is a thickness of material, usually one of several, that forms a distinct division, as **layers** in a cake, or **layers** in the earth.
6. A **volcano** is a mountain or hill that releases steam and molten rock from beneath the earth's surface. "Mt. Etna is an inactive **volcano** in Italy."
7. **Interurban** refers to a bus or other system that connects two or more cities.

8. A **motto** is a short statement expressing a belief or philosophy. "My **motto** is: 'Let honesty be your guide.'"

9. A **traveler's check** is a check issued by a bank or travel agency for the convenience of travelers.

10. The **rim** of the canyon is the upper edge. "The boys stood on the **rim** of the canyon."

11. A **dinosaur** is an extinct animal that lived millions of years ago.

12. **Fast food** is a type of food that can be quickly served and eaten, like hot dogs and hamburgers.

13. A **lunch stand** is a small restaurant, usually out of doors, that serves fast food.

3 VOCABULARY PRACTICE   *Fill in the blank spaces, using the vocabulary words above.*

1. The rocks in the canyon wall are arranged in horizontal _layer_.

2. I never carry cash when I travel, only _traveler's check_

3. When the wind blows away the soil, this process is called _Erosion_

4. The Grand _Canyon_, a national park in Arizona, is one mile deep.

5. Let's take the _Interurban_ bus from New York to Chicago.

6. My _motto_ is: "Look before you leap."

7. My uncle studies rocks and minerals. He's a _geologist_

8. The _dinosaur_ was an ancient reptile.

9. I'm in a hurry. Can we get some _Fast food_ for lunch?

10. Yes. We can get it at that _lunch stand_ over there.

4 VOCABULARY   *From the list below, select the word that best completes each sentence and write it in the blank space. Do not use any word more than once.*

deposits	research (learn)	major
booklet	Early Precambrian	boat ride

park ranger	soup	abyss
trail	unconscious	waiter
menu	suitcase	hawk
	dessert	

1. Let's take a _boat ride_ down the river.

2. Most travelers carry extra clothes in a ___suitcase___

3. To reach the Canyon, the boys walked along a ___trail___.

4. The ___Park ranger___ gave useful information to visitors.

5. The Canyon is a mile-deep ___abyss___

6. Geologists study rock ___deposits___ in the Canyon walls.

7. José selected his dinner from the restaurant ___menu___

8. The ___Waiter___ took his order.

9. To learn more about geology, do some ___research___ in the library.

10. The oldest layer in the Canyon is called ___Early Precambrian___

11. A ___hawk___ flew lazily overhead.

12. At dinner, the food often served first is called ___Soup___ , and the food

served last is ___dessert___

5 **SYNONYMS** *Rewrite the following sentences, replacing the word or phrase in italics with the best synonym from the word list. Do not use any synonym more than once.*

one billion	rapidly	flat	casual
cheap	trail	interurban	glanced (vista rapida)
rim	chasm	barely (apenas)	burst
gateway	dinosaurs	major	a million
scientific	Arizona	extinct	ice cream

1. The *canyon* was deep and wide. ___Chasm.___
2. The boys took *informal* clothes. ___Casual___

3. There are two *between-cities* bus lines in the U.S. *interurban*
4. Bus travel is relatively *inexpensive*. *cheap.*
5. The bones of *ancient reptiles* were found in the sand. *dinosaurs*
6. The best view is from the *edge* of the canyon. *trail*
7. José ordered *frozen milk* for dessert. *ice cream*
8. The sun set in an *explosion* of color. *burst*
9. One boy *looked quickly* at the menu. *rapidly glanced*
10. Dinosaurs are *no longer living*. *extinct*
11. Early Precambrian is a *technical* word. *scientific*
12. The boys could *hardly* wait. *barely*
13. The land was *level*. *flat*
14. They walked *quickly*. *rapidly*
15. These rocks are *1,000,000* years old. *one billion*

6 ***WORD-FORM CHART***   *Study the following words. Then do exercise 7.*

PARTICIPLE	NOUN	VERB	ADJECTIVE	ADVERB
	nature		natural	naturally
	geology geologist		geological	geologically
	impression	impress	impressive	impressively
studied studying	study student	study	studious	studiously
	knowledge	know	knowledgeable	knowledgeably
	history		historic	historically
	expense		expensive	expensively
	visibility		visible	visibly
	hunger	hunger	hungry	hungrily
	distance		distant	distantly

7 **WORD-FORM PRACTICE**   *In the blank space write the correct form of the italicized word.*

1. *distantly*   In the _distance_ the boys could see the opposite side of the canyon.

2. *history*   These are very _historic_ facts.

3. *knowledge*   The park ranger (was) very _knowledgeable_

4. *study*   Ibrahim was a _student_ from the Middle East.

5. *study*   Betty was both _studious_ and pretty.

6. *geology*   Several _geologists_ worked at the Canyon.

7. *geology*   They made _geological_ studies of the rocks.

8. *hunger*   The boys ate their dinner _hungrily_.

9. *hunger*   Are you _hungry_ right now?

10. *visible*   The _visibility_ was excellent.

11. *visibly*   Is the river _visible_ from here?

12. *expense*   Bus travel is not _expensive_ in the U.S.

13. *impression*   Her knowledge is _impressive_

14. *nature*   Babies learn to walk _Naturally_

15. *expensive*   Keep a record of your _expenses_

8 **READING COMPREHENSION**   *On the basis of the story, mark each sentence T if it is true or F if it is false.*

1. _F_ The boys approached the canyon from the ~~bottom~~ rim, near the river.

2. _F_ The visibility was poor on the day of their visit.

3. __F__ At dinnertime, neither boy was hungry.

4. __F__ The boys had fast food for dinner.

5. __F__ To communicate with each other, the boys spoke Spanish or Arabic.

6. __F__ The park ranger drove them around in a bus.

7. __T__ The canyon has six different climate zones.

8. __F__ Most modern zoos exhibit a dinosaur with the other animals.

9. __F__ The canyon is an astronomer's dream.

10. __T__ In the U.S., interurban buses carry more passengers than the railroads and airlines combined.

11. __T__ The rock layers are clearly visible in the canyon walls.

12. __F__ A volcano created the Grand Canyon.

9
ORAL PRACTICE I ***Things to Do at the Grand Canyon.*** *This exercise may be done as a class activity first, then continued by students working in pairs at their desks.*

I   A.   Procedure: *Ask questions about the picture (p.13), using time-sequence signals—first, next, then, last.*

Example	Student 1:	What would you like to do *first?*
	S 2:	*First* I'd like to take a bike ride.
	S 3:	What would you like to do *next?*
	S 4:	*Next* I'd like to take a nap.
	S 5:	*Then* what would you like to do?
	S 6:	*Then* I'd like to have a picnic.
	S 7:	What would you like to do *last?*
	S 8:	*Last* I'd like to collect fossils.

B.   *After the pattern has been learned, students should concentrate on the picture, and not look at the text. The teacher continues the practice, giving only the sequence signal—using the sequence signal by itself to cue the question and response.*

TEACHER: (first)
STUDENT 1: What would you like to do first?

C. Expansion Questions: *Using imagination and vocabulary from the story, the class invents additional questions and answers that elaborate on each of the ideas in A. The expansion questions can be about the number, size, type, color, or whatever is appropriate to the subject involved. Begin with the basic pattern.*

Example   Student 1:   What would you like to do first?
               S 2:   I'd like to take the mule trip first.
(Expansion)   S 3:   How many people are in your group?
               S 4:   There are six people in my group.
               S 5:   How many park rangers are in your group?

II. Class Game. *The practice can be turned into a game. Divide the class into small groups or teams. Have the teams take turns asking and responding to expansion questions. The first team to run out of a question or an answer loses the point. Mark the time and keep score.*

III. *For additional practice, students can transpose the questions to the past or future tense.*

Past Tense   S 1:   What did you do first yesterday?
               S 2:   Yesterday I took a bike ride first.
Future Tense   S 1:   What are you going to do first tomorrow?
               S 2:   Tomorrow I'm going to hunt for fossils first.

10 ORAL PRACTICE II   *Things to Avoid at the Grand Canyon*

As in Oral Practice I, this exercise should be done first by the class, then continued by students working together in pairs.

I A. Procedure: *Have a student ask a question about the picture in Oral Practice II (p.15). The response must turn the question into a statement, and add a "danger to avoid" from the picture.*

     Example   Student 1:   Would you like to take a hike?
                   S 2:   Yes, I would like to take a hike, but I wouldn't like to get lost.
                   S 3:   Would you like to have a picnic?
                   S 4:   Yes, I would like to have a picnic, but I wouldn't like to step on a snake.

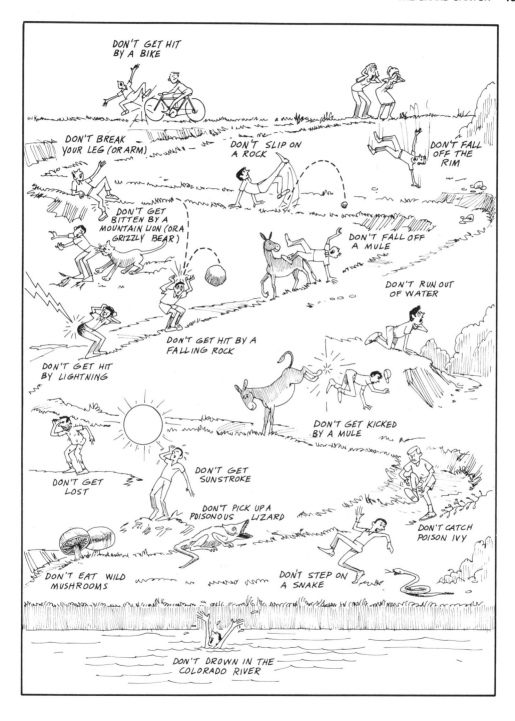

B. *After the pattern has been learned, the practice continues with the teacher (or a student) giving reduced word cues.*

Example TEACHER: Hike
    STUDENT 1: Would you like to take a hike?
     TEACHER: Be hit by lightning
      S 2: Yes, I would like to take a hike, but I wouldn't like to be hit by lightning.
     TEACHER: Have a picnic
      S 3: Would you like to have a picnic?
     TEACHER: Catch poison ivy
      S 4: Yes, I would like to have a picnic, but I wouldn't like to catch poison ivy.

II Class Game. *This game reviews the structure and vocabulary of Oral Practices I and II. The teams give and respond to reduced word cues, just as in the practices. To begin, the lead-off team gives a cue. The responding team must provide the correct pattern, and then give a cue in turn.*

Example
(question cue) Team 1: (*first*)
      Team 2: What would you like to do *first*?
(negative cue)   (not get lost)
      Team 3: I would like to take a hike *first*, but I wouldn't like to get lost.
(question cue)   (*next*)
      Team 4: What would you like to do *next*?
(negative cue)   (not start a fire)
      Team 5: I would like to have a picnic *next*, but I wouldn't like to start a fire.
(question cue)   (*then*)

Note: The lead-off teams must indicate in the cue whether they want the question (as in Practice I), or a negative answer (as in Practice II). The responding teams must recognize the cue and answer correctly. Mark the time and keep score.

11 **SKIT "LET'S GO"** *Students pretend to pack for a trip to the Canyon. Put the list of clothing and equipment on the board. Have the class add any missing items. Delete nonessentials. Pair students off to practice questions and answers. The best pairs can present their skits for the class.*

Ibrahim is going to take "casual" clothes and camping equipment. Which of the items below should he pack? How many and what kind of each should he take?

Clothing

heavy boots	raincoat	bedroom slippers
tuxedo	underwear	
one dozen yellow neckties	pajamas	
cotton socks	bathrobe	
wash-and-wear shirt	overcoat	
silk handkerchiefs	nylon jacket	
pants	wool sweater	

Equipment

flashlight	library books	extra food
canteen	picture of girl friend	tent
camera	snakebite kit	washcloth and towel
color film	phonograph records	blankets
matches	candles	

Question Practice: Answer in a complete sentence.

Are you going to take
$\begin{cases} a \\ any \\ some \\ a \ pair \ of \\ a \ suit \ of \end{cases}$ _____?

How many _____ are you going to take?

What color $\begin{cases} is \\ are \ your \end{cases}$ _____?

What size $\begin{cases} is \\ are \ your \end{cases}$ _____?

12 **CONTROLLED COMPOSITION** *Rewrite the selection below. Several ways are provided. Follow the directions in each step. Neatness counts, so write on every other line of your paper. If your handwriting needs improvement, do the penmanship practice on pp. 260-262.*

A Visit to the Grand Canyon

[1]Some overseas visitors come to the Grand Canyon each year. [2]They like the boat ride down the Colorado River. [3]They also like bird-watching and nature study. [4]The overnight mule trip is an unforgettable experience for them. [5]They

collect fossils and study the rock layers in the Canyon walls. [6]In the evening, they have dinner. [7]They order steak, and they also have ice cream. [8]There is plenty for them to do at the Canyon.

1. Copy the paragraph on your theme paper.
2. Rewrite the paragraph, changing "some overseas visitors" to "an overseas visitor".
3. Rewrite the paragraph changing the verbs to the past tense.

13 TOPICS FOR WRITING AND DISCUSSION

1. Pretend you are making a trip to the Grand Canyon. Tell what you would do first, what you would do second, third, and so on. Don't forget to tell about dinner in the restaurant.
2. Choose someplace of interest in your country that Americans should see. It can be ancient or modern, in a city or in the country. Explain why this place is interesting, and tell what there is to see and do there.
3. In your opinion, what is the most important place to visit in the world? Tell why you think so.
4. In a letter to a friend, describe an interesting trip you've taken.

14 DICTATION

1. The Grand Canyon is very impressive.
2. It is nearly a mile deep.
3. Geologists study rocks and soil erosion.
4. Visitors take a hike or ride a bike.
5. Buses are cheaper than trains.
6. The park rangers give helpful talks.
7. Take casual clothes and hiking boots.
8. Traveler's checks are safer than cash.
9. The dinosaur is extinct.
10. She likes vegetable soup and veal stew.

Two

AMERICAN GASTRONOMY

A Food Tour of the United States

Is it surprising that foods of great variety are found in a country as large and varied as the United States? Our total land mass occupies some 3,557,000 square miles, including Alaska and Hawaii. This area is divided into 50 states, of which the largest is Alaska and the smallest Rhode Island.

In this vast area almost every kind of climate and terrain occur. Parts of Alaska, for example, are located above the Arctic Circle, while some of our southern states enjoy year-round summer weather.

Not all these areas are equally suitable for agriculture. The Rockies, a rugged chain of mountains, occupy much of Colorado, Wyoming, Montana, Idaho, Utah, and New Mexico. Forests and deserts cover parts of other states. But most of the U.S. is flat and fertile. Approximately one-half of the country is situated in a rich agricultural area bounded by the Mississippi and Missouri rivers and the Great Lakes. Where there is good land, there are productive farms.

The climate also favors agriculture, though again there are wide variations. Temperatures above 100° Fahrenheit are not uncommon in Texas, Arizona, and southern California. And readings of 40° below zero have been reported in Alaska, North Dakota, and Montana. Generally, however, temperatures are moderate and favor the production of fruits, vegetables, and meat animals of many kinds.

How does the newcomer become acquainted with this aspect of American life? By making a food tour of the U.S.

(1)   One of the most intriguing features of American cooking is its variety. The traveler who crosses the U.S. by bus or by car, with stopovers in towns and cities along the way, will find the food as worthy of attention as the scenery—and full of unexpected surprises, too. For American cooking at its best is regional in character.

(2)   Except for turkey at Thanksgiving, no single dish has gained wide enough popularity in the U.S. to become a symbol for the country as a whole. There is no American eagle in our cookery. On the contrary, each region sets its table with a different specialty. These *spécialités de la region* capture the flavor and aroma and express the character of a particular locality. For instance, Cape Cod, a summer resort on the Atlantic Ocean, is famous for its clambakes, a seafood feast pulled ocean-fresh from the Atlantic and cooked over an outdoor fire on the beach. New Orleans is known for its jambalaya, a spicy dish of rice, ham, shrimp, and tomatoes. And Boston, where the winters are long and cold, is called "bean town" because of its baked beans, a blend of dried beans, salt pork, brown sugar, and molasses. Mixed in an iron pot and baked for hours in a slow oven, this dish is hearty and nutritious. Americans say, "It sticks to your ribs."

(3)   Being regional, these dishes feature the vegetables, fruits, meats, poultry, and seafood that are locally available. And since local conditions—the soil, climate, and topography—vary a great deal in the U.S., as might be expected in the world's fourth-largest country, the result is a national food menu on which most of the world's favorite foods are listed.

(4)   Seafood of all kinds is abundant in the states that border the oceans or possess lake and river systems. Shrimp, crab, and lobster, as well as fresh fish, are all mealtime favorites. Citrus fruit—oranges, grapefruit, lemons, and limes—are produced in Florida and California. The fruit groves in these states supply most of the frozen juice and sun-ripened fruit that grace the breakfast tables of the nation. Across the landlocked states in the Midwest stretch endless corn and wheat fields, rippling in the wind as far as the eye can see. These grains are used to make bread, cereal, and cooking oil. The region is called "the breadbasket of the nation." For vegetables, California is America's most bountiful state. It is first in the production of avocados, broccoli, asparagus, tomatoes, carrots, grapes, lettuce, peaches, and pears, and a cornucopia of other foods. Where is meat produced? In Texas, of course. That's where you can see all those tender roasts, steaks, and chops—"on the hoof."

(5)   True enough, all these foods are available at your local supermarket. But they have been canned, frozen, or packaged in some way and shipped many miles by rail or by truck. Wouldn't it be a treat—an adventure in gastronomy— to journey to the source, the point of origin, where the raw materials for great cooking begin? Pulled from the ocean or gathered farm fresh, this produce would be transformed by a local chef into a memorable dish fit for a king. After such a trip, what a gallery of memories the traveler would cherish!

(6)   I recall, for example, a marvelous breakfast I enjoyed at a hotel in Charleston, South Carolina. The food was served buffet style from a long table.

worthy = vale la pena   feast = festejo
clambakes = almejas   hearty = fuerte

This machine cuts the wheat, separates and bags the grain, all in one operation.

shipped = enviados

sticks = pegar   poultry = aves
Feature = presentar.   deal = repartir
stretch = alargar, estirar   tender = blando

In the supermarket, everything goes in the shopping cart, including the baby.

The first dish on the table was a bowl of grits, a southern specialty made of cornmeal. The waiter served the grits in big spoonfuls, heaping several pats of butter on top. Then came a large pan of salted beef in cream sauce. It was surrounded by dishes of spiced apples, bacon, and pork sausages. Eggs, sunny-side up or once-over-lightly, were next on the line. Beyond the eggs was a Virginia ham. Farther down the table were stacks of toast and plates of pancakes topped with maple syrup or honey and melted butter.

(7) Not only the excellence of the dishes made this breakfast memorable,

Crabs are cracked with a hammer and eaten with the fingers.

but also the graciousness with which it was served—southern hospitality at its best.

(8) The traveler who would like to sample the real flavor of American cooking must explore the country as a whole. There are five distinct regions in all. Each has its own characteristic dishes. There is the Northeast, stretching from Maine to Maryland, which is famous for its seafood; the South, which includes Mississippi, Alabama, Georgia, and neighboring states, where southern fried chicken, collard greens, cornbread, and black-eyed peas are popular; the Midwest, or plains states, of North and South Dakota, Nebraska, Illinois, and Kansas, which specialize in fine breads and pastries; the Mountain States of

Colorado, Montana, Wyoming, and Idaho, where wild game such as deer and pheasant are found; and the Southwest states of Arizona, New Mexico, and Texas, where barbecued food is a regional speciality. Since these last states border on Mexico, such dishes as enchiladas, tacos, tortillas, and chili con carne are also popular there.

(9)   Doesn't each of these regions deserve a visit by the dedicated traveler who enjoys good food?

Exercises

deserve = merecer

1 SCANNING   *To do this exercise, glance at the text for information, then, eyes up, give the response.*

1. What is one feature of American cooking? variety
2. How should the traveler cross the U.S.?
3. What will he find?
4. What is regional in character?
5. What food is eaten at Thanksgiving?
6. Which dish is a symbol for the country as a whole?
7. Where is Cape Cod?
8. What is Cape Cod famous for?
9. What is cooked over an outdoor fire?
10. What is New Orleans known for?
11. What are the ingredients of jambalaya?
12. Where are the winters long and cold?
13. What is Boston called?
14. Why is Boston called "bean town"?
15. What are the ingredients in baked beans?
16. What are these ingredients mixed in?
17. What do Americans say about this dish?
18. What do these regional dishes feature?
19. What varies a great deal in the U.S.?
20. What is the world's fourth-largest country?
21. Where is seafood abundant?
22. Name three kinds of seafood.
23. Where are citrus fruits produced?

24. What do the fruit groves supply?
25. Where are the wheat fields found?
26. What ripples in the wind?
27. What is this region called?
28. In what state are most vegetables grown?
29. Where is meat produced?
30. What is available at the supermarket?

2
VOCABULARY DEVELOPMENT Study the following words. The paragraph from
which each word comes is numbered. After studying these words, do exercise 3.

gastronomy (*title*)	**aroma** (*2*)	**bountiful** (*4*)
intriguing (*1*)	**hearty** (*2*)	**cherish** (*5*)
stopover (*1*)	**nutritious** (*2*)	
flavor (*2*)	**seafood** (*2*)	

1. **Gastronomy** is the art of good eating. A gourmet is a specialist in good food. But a gourmand is a greedy eater, a glutton.
2. To be **intriguing** is to be interesting, unusual.
3. A **stopover** is a pause in a trip, often for a night or more.
4. **Flavor** means taste.
5. **Aroma** means smell or odor. **Aroma** is applied to agreeable things like food or perfume.
6. **Hearty** food is satisfying and filling.
7. **Nutritious** food is good and healthy.
8. **Seafood** includes all types of fish and shellfish.
9. Something that is **bountiful** is abundant, in good supply.
10. To **cherish** something is to value it highly

cherish = apreciar

3
VOCABULARY PRACTICE Fill in the blank spaces, using the vocabulary words above.

1. After a short *stopover* in New York, we continued our journey the next day.

2. A *gourmet* is a lover of fine foods,

3. A _Gourmand_ overeats.

4. The taste of food is called its _Flavor_.

5. He valued his trip to Mexico and _cherished_ every memory.

6. Baked beans are very filling. They are a _Hearty_ dish.

7. The girl was interesting and unusual. He found her _Intriguing_.

8. When food promotes good health, it is _Nutritious_.

9. There are many fish in the ocean. They are a _bountiful_ source of food.

10. He likes clams, lobster, and other types of _seafood_.

4 VOCABULARY _From the list below, select the word that best completes each sentence and write it in the blank space. Do not use any word more than once._

seafood	aroma	flavor
buffet style	turkey	supermarket
tender	landlocked	adventure
maple syrup	citrus fruit	unforgettable
Midwest	breakfast	toast

1. My food tour was an _unforgettable_ experience.

2. In America _turkey_ is often the main dish at Thanksgiving.

3. Oysters, clams, and lobster are all types of _seafood_.

4. I buy meat, fruit, and vegetables at the _supermarket_.

5. A sweet topping for pancakes is called _maple syrup_.

6. A food tour is an _adventure_ in gastronomy.

7. Some states have no outlet to the sea. They are _landlocked_.

Salida

8. Oranges, lemons, and limes are types of _citrus fruit_.

9. Food is served __buffet__ *style* when you help yourself from a large table.

10. This meat is easy to chew. It is __tender__ *(blando)*

5

SYNONYMS   *Rewrite the sentences below, replacing the word or phrase in italics with the best synonym from the list. Do not use any synonym more than once.*

hospitality	sunny-side up	menu
sample	resort	once-over-lightly
memorable	gallery	clambake
border	topography	regions
grits	butter	raw

1. Puerto Rico has quite varied *land and water features.*

    Topography

2. Do not eat *uncooked* meat.

    raw

3. We asked the waiter for the *food list.*

    menu

4. Miami is a popular *vacation place.*

    resort

5. Some people like their eggs *with the yolk facing down.*

    once-over-lightly

6. Other people like their eggs *with the yolk facing up.*

    sunny side up

7. Let's have a *seafood cookout* on the beach.

    clambake

8. Some states *are next to* the ocean.

border

9. The U.S. can be divided into five *areas*.

regions

10. Before eating anything, you try a *small piece* first.

Sample

6

SYNONYM PRACTICE   *In the list below each sentence, find the synonym for the italicized word and draw a circle around it.*

1. Every visitor should *sample* American cooking.
   a. taste
   b. ignore
   c. produce

2. Seafood is *abundant* in the ocean.
   a. popular
   b. scarce
   c. plentiful

3. Baked beans are a *hearty* dish from Boston.
   a. fattening
   b. nutritious
   c. regional

4. Baked beans are made in an iron *pot*.
   a. farm tool
   b. kitchen container
   c. medical utensil

5. Regional dishes *feature* local produce.
   a. refuse
   b. ignore
   c. give prominence to

6. Regional dishes feature local *produce*.
   a. agricultural products
   b. industrial products
   c. medical products

o(c)

[ripol]

7. In the Midwest, wheat fields *ripple* in the wind.
- a. make wavelike motions
- b. stand motionless
- c. have a strong odor

ripple = very small wave [olas]

8. Each *locality* has dishes of its own.
- a. place
- b. people
- c. culture

9. One *intriguing* feature of America is its cooking.
- a. disturbing
- b. forgotten
- c. interesting

10. In the U.S. there are five *distinct* agricultural regions.
- a. vague
- b. occasional
- c. definite

7

ANTONYMS *For each word at the right, find the correct <u>antonym</u> in the list at the left. Write the antonym in the blank space. Do not use any antonym more than once.*

former *(Primer)*
easy
locality
ingredients
uncommon
forgettable
distribute
left unchanged
regional
nutritious
unpleasant
dwindle
capture
rudeness
cereal

1. forgettable memorable

2. rudeness graciousness

3. left unchanged transformed

4. distribute collect

5. capture escape

6. former latter *(ultimo)*

7. uncommon abundant

8. dwindle increase

9. easy difficult

10. unpleasant agreeable *(de aavedo)*

8 WORD-FORM CHART *Study the following words.*

PARTICIPLE	NOUN	VERB	ADJECTIVE	ADVERB
varied varying	variety	vary	various	variously
	region		regional	regionally
localized	locality	localize	local	locally
baked baking	bakery	bake		
	nutrition		nutritious	nutritiously
	abundance		abundant	abundantly
memorized memorizing	memory	memorize	memorable	memorably
	graciousness		gracious	graciously
dedicated dedicating	dedication	dedicate		
traveled traveling	traveler travel	travel		
mixed mixing	mixture	mix		

9 WORD-FORM PRACTICE *In the blank space, write the correct form of the italicized word.*

1. *gracious*   Food is served _graciously_ in the South.

2. *mix*   Pancakes are a _mixture_ of flour, eggs, and milk.

3. *local*   What is the best food in your _locality_ ?

4. *nutritious*   Do you believe in good _Nutrition_?

5. *travel*   The _traveler_ arrived late at the hotel.

6. *bakery*   How do you _bake_ bread?

7. *variety*   _Various_ types of seafood are good to eat.

8. *memory*   Visiting San Juan was a _memorable_ experience.

9. *nutrition*   Milk is a _nutritious_ food.

10. *abundant* There was an _abundant_ of food at the party.

10 **READING COMPREHENSION**   *Circle the letter (a, b, or c) that completes each sentence correctly.*

1. The best description of American cooking is that
   a. it has no individuality.
   b. it is the same all across the country.
   c. it is regional in character.

2. Cape Cod is a summer resort that is famous for
   a. seafood.
   b. wild game.
   c. southern fried chicken.

3. New Orleans is best known for its
   a. Alaska king crab.
   b. jambalaya.
   c. citrus fruit.

4. Which of the following are examples of seafood?
   a. oranges, grapefruit, lemons
   b. broccoli, asparagus, lettuce
   c. shrimp, crab, lobster

5. The Midwest is called the "breadbasket of the nation" because
   a. many baskets are made there.
   b. wheat grows abundantly there.
   c. vegetables grow abundantly there.

6. The state best known for its vegetables is
  a. California.
  b. New York.
  c. Florida.

7. The state best known for cattle and meat production is
  a. Oregon.
  b. Michigan.
  c. Texas.

8. The author enjoyed a delicious breakfast in
  a. Charleston.
  b. New York.
  c. New Orleans.

9. Which of the following states is *not* in the Northeast region?
  a. Maine
  b. Maryland
  c. Ohio

10. Which region makes a specialty of enchiladas, tortillas, and chili con carne?
  a. the Midwest
  b. the Southwest
  c. the Northwest

11 **USING A MENU** *Menu appears on pages 33 and 34.*

12 **ORAL PRACTICE** *Pretend you have gone to a good restaurant in New York and are ordering dinner. Choose a student to act the part of the waiter or waitress. He or she will take your order. Four students will play the parts of out-of-town visitors who want to eat. Everyone is very hungry and has a lot of money to spend. Practice the following questions and answers. Make substitutions of your choice from the menu for the items in parentheses. After practicing with the script a few times, go through the exercise without referring to the dialogue.*

WAITER: Good evening. May I take your order?
FIRST VISITOR: Not yet. We haven't made up our minds. While we're deciding, let's order some drinks.

(continue the practice on p. 35)

Menu

APPETIZER

Shrimp Cocktail	2.25	Melon Balls	.90
Oysters Rockefeller	2.50	Herring in Wine Sauce	1.50
Fruit Cup	1.50	Chicken Liver Pâté	1.75

Soup of the Day	1.00
Monday	Split Pea
Tuesday	Cream of Tomato
Wednesday	Corn Chowder
Thursday	Onion
Friday	Oyster Stew
Saturday	Manhattan Clam Chowder
Sunday	Chicken Noodle

MAIN COURSE

Yankee Pot Roast	4.50
T-Bone Steak	6.50
Pork Chops	3.75
Southern Fried Chicken	3.75
Leg of Lamb with Mint Sauce	4.50
Spareribs	3.75

FISH

Salmon Steak	3.25
Stuffed Flounder	3.75
Alaska King Crab	4.25
Lobster Tails	4.75
Scalloped Oysters	3.25
New England Steamed Clams	3.00

VEGETABLES   .50

Broccoli	Corn on the Cob	Baked Acorn Squash
Carrots	Boston Baked Beans	Spinach
Green Beans	Peas	Italian Eggplant

Steamed Rice   Mashed Potatoes

SALAD   1.00

Coleslaw	Caesar Salad	Three-Bean Salad
Lettuce and Tomato	Potato Salad	Vegetable Aspic
Cucumber	Chef's Salad	Cottage Cheese

Choice of Salad Dressing: Avocado, Blue Cheese, French, Mayonnaise,
        Russian, Thousand Island

DESSERT

Pie - -   Southern Pecan, Peach, Apple, Raisin 1.00
Cake - -   Chocolate, Devil's Food, Angel Food, Sponge...................... 1.00
Boston Cream Pie 1.50
Baked Custard 1.25
Bread Pudding .... .75
Cheesecake 2.25
Tapioca Pudding.. 1.25
Assorted Ice Cream - - Vanilla, Chocolate, Strawberry, Pineapple............. .75

BEVERAGE

Tea	.75	Milk	.65
Coffee	.75	Cocoa	.50
	Iced Tea .75		

DRINKS

Manhattan Cocktail	1.50	Bloody Mary	1.50
Martini Cocktail	1.25	Whiskey Sour	1.75
Scotch	1.75	Daiquiri	1.50
Gin and Tonic	1.50	Mint Julip	2.00
Domestic Beer	1.00	Imported Beer	2.00

WAITER: Very well. Would you like a cocktail?

FIRST VISITOR: Yes, bring me a martini on the rocks,* and make it extra dry.†

WAITER (*writing the order in a notebook*): Yes, sir. And you, Miss, what would you like?

SECOND VISITOR: I'll have a Bloody Mary, and do you have any cocktail crackers?

WAITER: Yes, Miss. I'll bring some. What would you like, sir?

THIRD VISITOR: I'll have a Scotch.‡ Make it a double. I feel like celebrating.

FOURTH VISITOR: I'll have a (*make a selection*).

WAITER: Are you ready to order now?

FIRST VISITOR: What would you recommend? I want American cooking.

WAITER: Why not have the Yankee Pot Roast? It's our special for today.

FIRST VISITOR: That sounds good. What goes with it?

WAITER: If you order the dinner, you get an appetizer, main course, three vegetables, salad, dessert, and beverage.

FIRST VISITOR: All right, I'll have (*make your selections*).

Second, Third, and Fourth Visitors also order.

---

13 **ORAL PRACTICE** *Dinner can also be ordered* à la carte. *Instead of taking a complete meal, one can order individual dishes separately. Practice having a student-waiter take an order from the class on the blackboard, totaling up the cost of each dish, and at the direction of the customer, figuring in the tip, which in this restaurant is 15 percent.*

---

14 **WORD PUZZLE** *The names of 20 common foods are hidden in the puzzle. How many foods from the list below the diagram can you find? The names read forward, backward,*

---

*On the rocks = a drink served with ice cubes.
†Extra dry = a martini made with gin and very little vermouth.
‡Whiskey can be ordered straight (by itself), with water, or with soda.

*up, or down, are always in a straight line and never skip letters. Two words—**apple** and **milk**—have been circled to get you started. Some letters may be used more than once, and some letters not used at all. Are you a good word detective? Happy hunting.*

A	P	L	E	T	T	U	C	E	P
P	E	A	C	H	R	S	L	I	I
P	A	W	Z	S	P	O	R	K	E
L	A	M	B	X	T	S	A	O	R
E	G	G	U	E	E	F	F	O	C
K	L	I	M	M	A	E	R	C	B
P	E	A	R	U	X	W	U	V	R
X	M	E	A	T	H	O	I	E	E
Y	O	R	A	N	G	E	T	A	A
U	N	P	R	R	S	Y	X	L	D

apple	fruit	orange
bread	lamb	pea
coffee	lemon	peach
cookie	lettuce	pear
cream	meat	pie
egg	milk	pork
roast	veal	

15 **CONTROLLED COMPOSITION**   *Rewrite the selection below. Two ways are provided. Follow the directions in each step.*

Soccer

[1]My favorite sport is soccer, a popular game around the world. [2]In fact, two soccer teams played an important match yesterday. [3]The home team wore a blue uniform. [4]Their opponents wore red.

[5]The Blues moved into position on the field. [6]They kicked off first. [7]The

referee gave the signal on his whistle. [8]Bozyk, the forward, gave the ball a tremendous kick. [9]It flew over the heads of the Reds. [10]Cardenas, who plays a rear position for the Reds, intercepted it. [11]He dribbled the ball up the field. [12]The Blues chased him. [13]The Reds blocked effectively, protecting Cardenas. [14]Cardenas made a run around the end. [15]He kicked the ball into the net for a goal. [16]The crowd stood and cheered. [17]Cardenas looked pleased.

1. Pretend the events are happening right now. Change the passage from the past to the present continuous, using the -ing verb form. Make the first verb-change in sentence 2, and use "today" instead of "yesterday."

> My favorite sport is soccer, a popular game around the world. In fact, two soccer teams *are playing* an important match today.

2. Sentence combining. Rewrite the selection, combining sentences 3 and 4, sentences 5 and 6, sentences 12 and 13, and sentences 15 and 16, with words like *and, but* or *so.*

16 *TOPICS FOR WRITING AND DISCUSSION*

1. Describe the various regions of your country and discuss the kinds of food that are produced there.
2. Explain how you would organize a picnic in your country. Tell what foods you would take and describe how you would prepare and serve them.
3. Do you cook seafood on the beach in your country? Tell how this is done.
4. Describe a memorable meal you have had in the United States.
5. Explain how to prepare your favorite dish.
6. What was the worst meal you ever ate? Tell why.

17 *DICTATION*

1. American cooking is regional in character.
2. Cape Cod is a summer resort on the Atlantic Ocean.
3. Because of its baked beans, Boston is called "bean town."
4. This dish is hearty and nutritious.
5. Americans say, "It sticks to your ribs."

6. Seafood is abundant in the oceans.
7. Broccoli and asparagus grow in California.
8. Most foods are available in the supermarket.
9. I enjoyed a marvelous breakfast in Charleston.
10. The South specializes in fried chicken and black-eyed peas.

Three

THE STORY OF JAZZ

Music comes in many forms; most countries have a style of their own. Poland has its polkas. Hungary has its czardas. Brazil is famous for the bossa nova, Caribbean countries for the merengue, and Argentina for the tango. The U.S. is known for jazz, a completely original type of music that has gained worldwide popularity.

(1)   Jazz is America's contribution to popular music. In contrast to classical music, which follows formal European traditions, jazz is spontaneous and free-form. It bubbles with energy, expressing the moods, interests, and emotions of the people. Brash, uninhibited, exciting, it has a modern sound. In the 1920s, jazz sounded like America. And so it does today.

(2)   The origins of this music are as interesting as the music itself. Jazz was invented by American Negroes, or blacks, as they are called today, who were brought to the southern states as slaves. They were sold to plantation owners and forced to work long hours in the cotton and tobacco fields. This work was hard and life was short. When a Negro died, his friends and relatives formed a procession to carry the body to the cemetery.

(3)   In New Orleans, a band often accompanied the procession. On the way to the cemetery the band played slow, solemn music suited to the occasion. But on the way home the mood changed. Spirits lifted. Everybody was happy.

King Oliver's Jazz Band in Chicago, about 1922, with Louis Armstrong on trumpet.

Death had removed one of their number, but the living were glad to be alive. The band played happy music, improvising on both the harmony and the melody of the tunes presented at the funeral. This music made everyone want to dance. It was an early form of jazz. But there were other influences, too.

(4)   Music has always been important in Negro life. Coming mainly from West Africa, the blacks who were brought to America already possessed a rich musical tradition. This music centered on religious ceremonies in which dancing, singing, clapping, and stamping to the beat of a drum were important forms of musical and rhythmic expression. As these people settled in to their new life on the plantations of the South, music retained its importance. In the fields, they made up work songs. Singing made the hard work go faster. And as the people were converted to Christianity, they composed lovely spirituals, which have become a permanent part of American music.

(5)   Another musical form that contributed to jazz was the blues. Blues

songs, such as W. C. Handy's "St. Louis Blues," always describe something sad—an unhappy love affair, a money problem, bad luck. To this day, the expression "feeling blue" means being sad or depressed.

(6) In fact, there was hardly any activity or social event that could not be set to music. Weddings, births, christenings, funerals, picnics, parades—all had their musical accompaniment.

(7) All of this became more important after the American Civil War (1861–1865). By then the Negroes had gained their freedom and were ready for a new type of music, one that would preserve their musical traditions but be fast and happy to express their newfound freedom. They wanted something they could play as professional musicians for both black and white audiences. Jazz was the answer. It combined themes from Negro work songs, spirituals, and blues, set to a fast beat, with the musicians improvising as they went along, like the funeral marching bands. But one element was still needed to make this music popular—a city.

(8) Jazz needs bars, cafés, and dance halls, and it needs people in search of uninhibited entertainment. These conditions were provided in the honky-tonk sections of New Orleans, a busy seaport on the Gulf of Mexico. During the day this city was businesslike; at night it wanted fun.

(9) New Orleans, having belonged first to France, then to Spain, then to France again, was very cosmopolitan and sophisticated about entertainment. When the city passed to the United States in 1803 as part of the Louisiana Purchase, a tolerant view of vice was part of its history. By the 1900s, New Orleans had become a commercial and trading center for the world. Ships of every nation docked there, and in the evening the sailors went into town. Soldiers from a large army camp nearby also visited the city looking for fun. New Orleans provided plenty of gaiety and bright lights in a disreputable district called Storyville, which was filled with bars, dance halls, and bordellos. Each of these places had its own orchestra, and this helped popularize the new music. Jazz was on its way.

(10) In those early days the orchestras were small. They usually consisted of seven instruments—a trumpet, a cornet, a clarinet, a piano, a trombone, a banjo, and a set of drums. Each was played by a specialist, a real virtuoso. Baby Dodds played the drums, for instance, and King Oliver the cornet. This music was not written down. In fact, much of it was improvised on the spot. To be good, a musician had not only to remember his part but also to be able to invent new variations on the spur of the moment. That is what makes songs like "Beale Street Blues," "Basin Street Blues" (both named after streets in New Orleans), and "When the Saints Go Marching In" so exciting. They were never played exactly the same way twice.

(11) Jazz belongs to the people, but popular taste is changeable. Jazz had to keep up-to-date. Over the last half century it has changed many times in form, style, and tempo. Each change added something new. In today's usage, "jazz" includes not only Dixieland, the original name for this music, but also bepop,

The French Quarter in New Orleans has bars, restaurants, and other places of entertainment.

progressive jazz, swing, and boogie-woogie. Rock 'n' roll, while not strictly a form of jazz, is nevertheless an outgrowth of it. All are imaginative and improvisational, with great freedom in harmony and instrumentation. The late jazz pianist Jelly Roll Morton summed up jazz as "playing more music than you can put on paper."

Exercises

1 **SCANNING** *To do this exercise, glance at the text for information, then, eyes up, give the response.*

1. What is America's contribution to popular music? Jazz
2. Which music follows European traditions? Classical Music
3. Which music is spontaneous? Jazz

4. What does jazz express? *Moods, interests, emotion of the people*

5. What kind of sound does jazz have? *Modern sound*

6. What did jazz sound like in the 1920s? *America*

7. What are as interesting as the music? *The origins*

8. Who invented jazz? *American Negroes*

9. Where were the slaves brought? *Southern states*

10. Where were the slaves forced to work? *Plantations*

11. What was hard? *the work*

12. What was short? *the life*

13. What happened when a Negro died? *They had a procession to carry the body*

14. What accompanied the procession? *the band*

15. What did the band play on the way to the cemetery? *slow, solemn music*

16. What happened to the mood on the way home? *Spirit lifted suited to the occasion*

17. What lifted? *Spirits*

18. Who was happy? *Everybody* *Every body was happy*

19. What had death removed? *one of their number*

20. Who was glad to be alive? *the living*

21. What did the band play? *happy music*

22. What did the band improvise? *armony and melody*

23. What did this music make everyone want to do? *Dance*

24. What has always been important in Negro life? *Music*

2
VOCABULARY DEVELOPMENT *Study the following words. The paragraph from which each word comes is numbered. After studying these words, do exercise 3.*

brash (*1*)	**improvise** (*3*)	**honky-tonk** (*8*)
uninhibited (*1*)	**melody** (*3*)	**sophistication** (*9*)
spontaneous (*1*)	**harmony** (*3*)	**cosmopolitan** (*9*)

1. Brash means something new that is unafraid to break traditions (possibly it doesn't know what the traditions are), tactless, hasty, and a little impudent. For example, it is **brash** to express an opinion without thinking about it.

2. When we act without restraint, we are **uninhibited.** Someone at a party who dances wildly and laughs and talks as freely as he or she wants is **uninhibited.**

3. An action is **spontaneous** when it hasn't been planned in advance but occurs at the moment on an impulse.

4. In music, to **improvise** is to compose and perform at the same time. "The young man was asked to accompany the singer. Since he did not know the music, he had to **improvise** on the piano."

5. The **melody** is the tune or familiar part of the song. It can be played or sung by itself.

6. The **harmony** is the accompaniment to the melody. It adds richness, fullness, color, and beauty and is usually not played by itself.

7. The **honky-tonk** part of a city is where the bars, cafés, and dance halls are located.

8. **Sophistication** is a quality sought by many people. People are **sophisticated** when they know the world and how to behave, especially in society.

9. A city is **cosmopolitan** when it contains a blend of cultures and people from all over the world. In the United States, New York, San Francisco, and New Orleans are our most **cosmopolitan** cities.

3 VOCABULARY PRACTICE   *Fill in the blank spaces, using the vocabulary words above.*

1. Jack's actions were always quick and unplanned. They were completely
   spontaneous

2. Linda was a girl who had been everywhere and knew everyone. She was very
   sophisticated

3. Betty did not know the music. She would have to _improvise_.

4. When asked to play music at a party, Betty always played the _harmony_ while everyone else sang the melody.

5. Paris, with its mixed population, is very _cosmopolitan_

6. Paul did not understand the discussion, but he made a suggestion anyway. His suggestion was _brash_. Fortunately, it met with approval.

7. Times Square, with its bars, cheap movies, and low entertainment, is the _honky-tonk_ section of New York.

8. "Let Alice play the harmony on the piano; I'll play the _melody_ on the trumpet," Jack said.

9. Jane had had several drinks and felt very *uninhibited*, so she took off her shoes and danced with everyone else's husband.

4 *MUSICAL INSTRUMENTS* *Musical instruments are of three general types—wind instruments, stringed instruments, and percussion instruments.*

Wind Instruments

Wind instruments are held to the mouth to be played. They include:

the trumpet	the tuba	the flute
the cornet	the clarinet	the oboe
the saxophone	the French horn	the bassoon
the trombone		

cuerda

Stringed Instruments

Stringed instruments are played with a bow or they are plucked (played with the fingers). Some stringed instruments may be played both ways. Stringed instruments include:

the violin	the cello	the guitar
the viola	the bass viol	the banjo

The piano is a special kind of stringed instrument.

Percussion Instruments

Percussion instruments are struck to produce a sound. They include:

the cymbals	the drum
the xylophone	the tambourine

All these instruments have been used at one time or another by jazz musicians.

5
ORAL PRACTICE ON MUSICAL INSTRUMENTS, I *Practice the names of the musical instruments by asking questions and giving responses. Study the following example:*

TEACHER: Is the trumpet a stringed instrument?
STUDENT: No, the trumpet is a wind instrument.
TEACHER: Is the violin played with a bow?
STUDENT: Yes, the violin is played with a bow.
TEACHER: Is the guitar played with a bow?
STUDENT: No, the guitar is plucked (played with the fingers).
TEACHER: Is the oboe a percussion instrument?
STUDENT: No, the oboe is a wind instrument.
TEACHER: Are the drums played with the mouth?
STUDENT: No, the drums are struck to produce sound.

Continue this practice with the other instruments.

6
ORAL PRACTICE ON MUSICAL INSTRUMENTS, II *Discuss the sounds musical instruments make, by asking questions and giving responses. Use words like* soft, loud, pleasant, unpleasant, harsh, *and* agreeable. *For instance:*

Practice A

1. Does the violin make a loud or a harsh sound?
2. Does the violin make a harsh or a sweet sound?

Continue the practice with other instruments.

Practice B

1. Is the violin as loud as the trumpet?
2. Is the piano as interesting as the oboe?

Continue the practice with other instruments.

7
ORAL PRACTICE ON MUSICAL INSTRUMENTS, III *Discuss the use of musical instruments by asking questions and giving responses. For instance:*

1. Is the violin used in a marching band?
2. Is the piano used in a military band?

3. Is the trumpet used in a jazz band?

4. Is the violin used in a symphony orchestra?

5. Are the drums used in a dance band?

6. Can you play a love song on the tuba?

7. Can you play the melody on the drums?

Continue the practice with similar questions and other instruments.

8 VOCABULARY *From the list below, select the word that best completes each sentence and write it in the blank space. Do not use any word more than once.*

tolerant	clapping	gained
musician	wedding	christening
honky-tonk	spirituals	banjo
harmony	tune	polka
beat	spontaneous	marching band
funeral	instrument	piano
befitting	sophisticated	

1. A trumpet is a wind _instrument_

2. Eileen got married on Sunday, so Sunday was her _wedding_ day.

3. A _christening_ is the ceremony of naming a baby in church. [cristening]

4. When someone dies, we make _funeral_ arrangements. aweglo

5. A _musician_ is a person who plays an instrument.

6. Bars and cafés were located in the _honky-tonk_ sections of New Orleans.

7. Linda was worldly-wise and knew how to behave in any situation. She was very _sophisticated_. sabudonadelmundo

8. _Clapping_ is making a sound with the hands.

9. _Spirituals_ are traditional religious songs composed by Negro slaves.

10. Music is _spontaneous_ when it is instinctive and unrehearsed. sin practicar

11. The main part or melody of a song is called the _tune_.

beat = rítmo

12. The accompaniment to the melody is called the ___harmony___.

13. The blacks from West Africa danced to the ___beat___ of a drum.

14. A ___piano___ is an instrument with 88 keys.

15. New Orleans had a ___tolerant___ attitude toward entertainment.

9

SYNONYMS   *Rewrite the following sentences replacing the word or phrase in italics with the best synonym from the word list. Do not use any synonym more than once.*

alguien que

late = (muere) en el siglo

origins	plantation	depressed
docked	late	desired (buscar)
plantations	improvise	procession
drum	brash	Hollywood
solemn	clapping	trumpet

depressed
1. Carmen felt *blue* all day. *desired*
2. The slaves *longed for* a better life.
procession 3. A *line of people* formed for the wedding.
late 4. The *recently deceased* Jelly Roll Morton was respected by everyone.
plantations 5. Slaves worked on *large farms* in the South.
clapping 6. *Striking the hands together* makes a rhythmic sound.
improvise 7. Jazz musicians *make up* the music as they play.
8. Church music is usually *serious*. *solemn*
9. Ships frequently *landed* in New Orleans. *docked*
10. The *beginnings* of jazz are interesting.
    origins

10

READING COMPREHENSION   *On the basis of the story, mark each of the following sentences T if it is true or F if it is false.*

1. __F__ In most respects, jazz is very similar to classical music.

2. __F__ Jazz was first played in Africa.

3. __F__ To celebrate the death of a slave, happy music was played on the way to the cemetery.

*spic
prohibidos*

4. _F_ Negroes were forbidden to sing in the fields by the plantation owners.

5. _T_ Blues songs *always* describe something sad.

6. _T_ Music was played for all of the following events: weddings, picnics, christenings.

7. _F_ When Negroes invented jazz, they wanted a musical form that was entirely outside their traditions.

8. _T_ In the early 1900s, New Orleans was primarily a commercial and trading seaport.

9. _F_ Originally, jazz was played in churches. *(was played in funeral)*

10. _T_ In modern usage, jazz also includes swing and boogie-woogie.

11 PREPOSITIONS   *Insert the correct preposition in each blank space.*

1. Jazz expresses the moods __*of*__ the people.

2. This music was played _____ virtuosos.

3. Work songs were sung _____ the fields.

4. Music provides relief _____ the hard work.

5. Music has always been important __*to*__ the lives __*of*__ this people.

6. Solemn music was played __*on*__ the way __*to*__ the cemetery.

7. The relatives felt sorry __*about*__ the deceased.

8. Ships __*of*__ every nation docked __*in*__ New Orleans.

9. The sailors went __*into*__ town looking __*for*__ fun.

10. The blacks brought a rich musical tradition _____ them _____ Africa.

12 ARTICLES   *Use* the, a, *or* an *if necessary.*

1. _____The_____ jazz was invented by _____the_____ blacks.

2. _____The_____ origins of this music go back to _____a_____ turn of _____the_____ century.

3. Jazz was _____an_____ invention outside _____the_____ European traditions.

4. Negro slaves sang and whistled _____ work songs and _____ spirituals.

5. Jazz bubbles with _____ energy. It expresses _____ moods of

   _____ people.

6. _____ blacks changed their musical traditions into _____ new idiom.

7. _____ deceased was accompanied to _____ cemetery by his friends.

8. When there was _____ wedding, _____ christening, _____

   funeral, _____ picnic, or _____ parade, _____ music was wanted.

13 WORD-FORM CHART   *Study the following words.*

PARTICIPLE	NOUN	VERB	ADJECTIVE	ADVERB
contributed contributing	contribution	contribute		
	profession		professional	professionally
	tradition		traditional	traditionally
popularized popularizing	popularity	popularize	popular	popularly
	spontaneity		spontaneous	spontaneously

PARTICIPLE	NOUN	VERB	ADJECTIVE	ADVERB
	seriousness		serious	seriously
punished punishing	punishment	punish		
improvised improvising	improvisation	improvise		
depressed depressing	depression	depress		
imagined imagining	imagination	imagine	imaginative	imaginatively
	instrument instrumentation		instrumental	

(14) **WORD-FORM PRACTICE**   *In the blank space, insert the correct form of the italicized word.*

1. *contribute*   Blacks made an important ___contribution___ to popular music.

2. *profession*   The doctor was very ___professional___ in his manner.

3. *punishment*   Should you ___punish___ a child if he is bad?

4. *spontaneously*   Jane was ___spontaneous___ and uninhibited.

5. *improvise*   ___Improvisation___ is very important in jazz.

6. *serious*   Some people take jazz very ___seriously___.

7. *traditional*   Classical music follows European ___tradition___.

8. *punish*   "Let the ___punishment___ fit the crime" is a Biblical rule.

9. *imagination*   Can you ___imagine___ what life used to be like in New Orleans?

10. *instrumentation*   Can you play an ___instrument___?

11. *popular*   Frank Sinatra has _popularized_ many songs.

12. *depression*   Betty felt very _depressed_ this morning.

13. *tradition*   _traditional_ songs are best.

14. *contribution*   Which charity do you _contribute_ to?

15. *imagination*   Jazz is _imaginative_ and free-flowing.

15 IDIOMS AND SPECIAL EXPRESSIONS   *Circle the letter (a, b, or c) in front of the word that completes the sentence correctly.*

1. Jazz had to keep _____ to-date.
   a. down
   b. away
   c. up-

2. This music was improvised on the _____ of the moment.
   a. brink
   b. spur
   c. time

3. On the _____ home, the musicians played lively tunes.
   a. way
   b. back
   c. ago

4. When I'm sad, I feel _____.
   a. green
   b. red
   c. blue

5. Rock 'n' _____ was an outgrowth of jazz.
   a. bread
   b. run
   c. roll

6. The slaves made _____ work songs.
   a. down
   b. away
   c. up

7. _____ fact, most activities can be set to music.
   a. on
   b. in
   c. from

8. We will iron _____ our problems later.
   a. out
   b. from
   c. in

9. No one set _____ to invent jazz.
   a. out
   b. in
   c. from

10. This music was not written _____.
   a. down
   b. from
   c. to

16
CONTROLLED COMPOSITION   *Rewrite the selection below. Follow the directions in each step.*

Jazz

¹Jazz is *music*. ²It was *played* by *musicians* who *worked* in *bars* in New Orleans. ³At that time, New Orleans was a *city*. ⁴The *people* there liked *fun*. ⁵They liked *to talk* and *dance*. ⁶*Music* will always be a part of *life*.

1. Rewrite the passage. Make it more interesting and colorful by attaching adjectives or adverbs, as required, to *music* (in sentence 1), *played* (2), *musicians* (2), *worked* (2), *bars* (2), *city* (3), *people* (4), *fun* (4), *to talk* (5), *dance* (5), *music* (6) and *life* (7).

2. When the compositions are finished, have students put their work on the blackboard. Discuss the choice of words that were used or might have been used.

17 TOPICS FOR WRITING AND DISCUSSION

1. "America was receptive to jazz because the country, like the music, was brash, uninhibited, and exciting." Keeping in mind what these adjectives mean, write an essay in which you agree or disagree with this statement.
2. Which style of music do you prefer—Latin American, operatic, symphonic, military, jazz, rock 'n' roll, or some other? Explain why this style appeals to you.
3. Your school is planning to hold a dance. You are a member of the dance committee and have been asked to hire a band and make all the arrangements. What food, social activities, and room decorations would you prepare? Describe all the arrangements you would make.
4. Describe the steps that are required to learn to play an instrument. Number each step in the proper order—first, second, third, and so on. These steps should be so clear that someone else could learn the instrument from your description.
5. Describe the best dance you ever attended.
6. Describe the popular music of your country.
7. Who is your favorite musician? Tell why you like him or her.

18 DICTATION

1. The procession conveyed the deceased to the cemetery.
2. The band played solemn music.
3. This music befitted the seriousness of the occasion.
4. The African blacks combined singing, dancing, and clapping in their religious ceremonies.
5. Sing the blues when you are depressed.
6. Jazz is usually played by professional musicians.
7. New Orleans was a cosmopolitan city.
8. Ships docked there frequently.
9. The city provided gaiety and bright lights.
10. Is the trombone, the banjo, or the clarinet your favorite instrument?

Four

LOUIS ARMSTRONG

A Jazz Immortal

At the turn of the century, when jazz was born, America had no prominent music of its own. The popular operas of that day were all by European composers, and so were the symphonies. Dance music consisted of fox trots and old-fashioned waltzes that belonged to an earlier era. But times were changing. Americans were building railroads and steamboats, factories and power plants. Cities were pulsating with vitality. A new world was emerging, and it needed music with a modern beat and a lively sound. The times were just right for jazz. Of all the men associated with this music, none is more famous than Louis Armstrong. This is his story.

(1)   No one knows exactly when jazz was invented, or by whom. But it began to be heard in the early 1900s. Jazz was a new kind of music, for America and the world, and New Orleans was its birthplace.

(2)   Who were the jazz pioneers? Most were blacks. This music was not written down, and at first only blacks played it. It was hard for white musicians to learn the new style. But soon they, too, were playing jazz.

(3)   The popularity of this music spread. From New Orleans it traveled up the Mississippi to Chicago, then to Kansas City and New York. By the 1920s there were many jazz musicians, both black and white. Many were outstanding; some were brilliant. One man was better than the rest. His name was Louis Armstrong.

Bing Crosby and Louis Armstrong were friends who appeared together in movies and on the stage.

(4)   The career of Louis Armstrong spans jazz history, from its beginnings in New Orleans through the many developments of later years. He was a born musician. He combined talent with a great deal of hard work. He also had a good sense of humor and a big, good-natured grin. These personal qualities were invaluable in his rise to fame. After he became well known, he traveled around the world. Everyone, it seemed, wanted to hear Louis play. But life was not always easy, especially at the beginning.

(5)   Louis Armstrong was born in 1900 in a run-down section of New Orleans. His father was illiterate and his mother could barely read. When Louis was still a kid, his parents separated, and Louis lived with his mother. How hard their life was can readily be imagined. And yet Louis smiled through everything. He later wrote, "My whole life has been happiness. Life was there for me and I accepted it. Whatever came out has been beautiful to me. I love everybody."

grin — sonrisa

(6)   As a kid, Louis had to work hard. He sold newspapers on the streets and was a loader in a coal yard. Of formal education, he had little. Sometimes there was not much food in the house. But there was music everywhere, and it was free. There were parades and dances and singing in the streets. Little Louis absorbed it all.

(7)   Then he got into trouble. In 1912 he was arrested for carrying a gun. It was a childish prank, but he was sent to the Colored Waifs' Home, a school for wayward boys. While there, as a reward for good behavior, he was taught to play the cornet. This was the turning point in his life. After his release from the home, Louis got a job playing in a jazz band.

malcom

(8)   For a few years Louis played in the bars and cabarets of New Orleans and on the riverboats that ran up and down the Mississippi. Then in 1922, when Louis was 22 years old, he received an invitation from King Oliver, then the leader of a popular jazz band in Chicago. King Oliver asked Louis to join him in the North. Louis did. It was the first time he had been away from home, and it was another important step in his career.

(9)   As a newcomer to the band, Louis's job was to back up the others, for jazz is above all a group effort. From time to time, he and King Oliver played duets on the cornet or the trumpet for songs like "Them There Eyes" or "Bugle Call Rag." Louis already had a style of his own. Even at this early stage, many believed he could outperform King Oliver, the star of the band. Now Louis began to attract attention from the public, the critics, and, best of all, from other musicians. Everyone loved to hear him play.

(10)   In the 1920s Louis played with different bands, sometimes in New York, sometimes in Chicago. He began to make phonograph records. These recordings helped to spread his musical reputation. People all around the country who were unable to see him in person could enjoy his music on records. Pretty soon Louis had a band of his own called the Hot Five. And hot it was. No one could play the trumpet like Louis. He invented ways to embellish a melody, playing each note so hot and fast and with such feeling that it had tremendous impact on the audience. Sometimes he put down his horn and sang. Instead of words, he made up strange sounds, using his voice like an instrument. It all blended together perfectly. His sense of comedy, his physical appearance and mannerisms, and his extraordinary vocal style all contributed to his great success.

(11)   Louis toured the country with his band, and in the 1930s he made movies in Hollywood. After that, Louis was not only a national but an international figure. He traveled to Europe and played jazz for the king of England. Sponsored by the Pepsi-Cola Company, Louis made an extended tour of Africa, appearing before large crowds in Nigeria, the Congo, Uganda, and other African countries. Everywhere he went, Louis was a sensation.

(12)   The years rolled by, but Louis never gave up his music or lost his popularity. He was a jazz immortal. Louis Armstrong died on July 6, 1971. Thousands of people attended his funeral. As the procession neared his house, a small boy held up a sign. It read, "We love you, Louis."

Exercises

1 **SCANNING** *To do this exercise, glance at the text for information, then, eyes up, give the response.*

1. When was jazz invented?
2. Who invented jazz?
3. When did Americans begin to hear jazz?
4. What kind of music was it?
5. What was the birthplace of jazz?
6. Who were the jazz pioneers?
7. Was this music written down?
8. Who was able to play this music first?
9. Then who learned to play this music?
10. What happened to the popularity of this music?
11. To which cities did this music travel?
12. By what time were there many jazz musicians?
13. Which musician was better than all the rest?
14. What does the career of Louis Armstrong span?
15. Who was a born musician?
16. What did he combine?
17. What else did he have?
18. What was invaluable in his rise to fame?
19. What did he do after he became well known?
20. Who wanted to hear Louis play?
21. What was not always easy?
22. When was Louis born?
23. Where was Louis born?
24. Who was illiterate?
25. Who could barely read?
26. When did his parents separate?
27. Whom did Louis live with?
28. What was their life like?
29. What did they say about his early life?
30. When did Louis have to work hard?
31. What work did he do first?

32. Then what work did he do?
33. How much education did he have?
34. Was there always food in the house?
35. Where did he hear music?
36. How much did the music cost?
37. What did he see in the streets?
38. What happened to Louis in 1912?
39. When did Louis get into trouble?
40. What kind of prank was it?
41. Where was Louis sent?
42. How was he rewarded for good behavior?
43. What did Louis do after he was released from the Home?
44. Where did Louis play at first?
45. How old was Louis in 1922?
46. What happened to him in that year?
47. Who was King Oliver?
48. Who asked Louis to join him in the North?
49. As a newcomer to the band, what was Louis's job?
50. How often did he and King Oliver play duets?

VOCABULARY DEVELOPMENT *Study the following words. The paragraph from which each word comes is numbered. After studying these words, do exercise 3.*

jazz (*1*)
pioneer (*2*)
outstanding (*3*)
talent (*4*)
run-down (*5*)
reward (*7*)
pranks (*7*)
career (*8*)
duets (*9*)
embellish (*10*)

1. **Jazz** is music based on black spirituals, blues, and work songs.
2. A **pioneer** is someone who does something for the first time.
3. To be **outstanding** is to be especially good at something.
4. **Talent** is a special ability one has for something.
5. A section of the city that is **run-down** is in poor condition.
6. A **reward** is something given to honor merit, service or achievement.
7. **Pranks** are tricks or jokes played on someone.
8. A **career** is an occupation or profession.

(Duetos) **9. Duets** are pieces of music performed by two people.

10. To **embellish** is to make something fancy.

3 *VOCABULARY PRACTICE* *Fill in the blank spaces, using the vocabulary words above.*

1. Louis was born in a _run-down_ section of town.

2. Being a musician was the _career_ he would follow all his life.

3. He and his friend King Oliver frequently played _duets_ in the band.

4. As a _reward_, Louis was taught to play the cornet.

5. He was _oustanding_ in his field.

6. He learned how to _embellish_ a note.

7. Louis was a _pioneer_ in his field.

8. Full of fun, Louis often played _Pranks_ on his friends.

9. The new music was called _Jazz_.

10. Louis had a great _talent_ for music.

4 *VOCABULARY* *From the list below, select the word that best completes each sentence and write it in the blank space. Do not use any word more than once.*

zest	kid	extended
prank	outstanding	birthplace
sponsored	newcomer	absorbed
composer	glowing	reputation
riverboat	Chicago	blend

1. As a _kid_, Louis sold newspapers and worked in a coal yard.

2. New Orleans was his _birthplace_.

3. Louis had a _____zest_____ for life.

4. Everyone considered his playing _____outstanding_____

5. Carrying a gun was a childish _____prank_____.

6. Louis _____absorbed_____ everything he heard and saw.

7. Phonograph records enhanced his musical _____reputation_____.

8. When Louis first arrived in Chicago, he was a _____newcomer_____ in King Oliver's band.

9. The Pepsi-Cola Company _____sponsored_____ his tour.

10. Louis made an _____extended_____ tour of the world.

5
SYNONYMS *Rewrite the following sentences, replacing the word or phrase in italics with the best synonym from the following list. Do not use any synonym more than once.*

reputation	musician	wayward
rolled by	career	the pioneers
talent	illiterate	preeminent
squalid	band	turning point
an impact	spans	embellish
cabaret	mannerisms	toured
mentor	audience	

1. His *distinctive behavior* attracted attention.

mannerisms

2. The years *passed quickly*.

rolled by

3. *Those who go first* make the most important discoveries.

The pioneers

4. Eugene chose medicine as his *lifework*.

career

5. Louis undoubtedly had a *special ability* for music.

talent

6. King Oliver was Louis's *wise and faithful friend*.

mentor

7. Louis *traveled all over* the world.

toured

8. The man was *unable to read or write*.

illiterate

9. She was born in a *run-down* part of town.

squalid

10. He was sent to a home for *delinquent* boys.

wayward

11. Learning to play the cornet was the *most important event* in Louis's life.

turning point

12. Louis learned how to *dress up* a melody.

embellish

13. His music had *a strong effect* on his listeners.

an impact

14. They met at a *bar that had musical entertainment*.

cabaret

15. The career of a successful man often *stretches across* several decades.

spans (bridge)

6

WORD-FORM CHART *Study the following words.*

PARTICIPLE	NOUN	VERB	ADJECTIVE	ADVERB
invented inventing	invention inventor	invent	inventive	inventively
personalized personalizing	personality	personalize	personal	personally
glowed glowing	glow	glow		
arrested arresting	arrest	arrest		
	child		childish	childishly
invited inviting	invitation	invite		
recorded recording	record recording	record		
blended blending	blend	blend		
immortalized immortalizing	immortality immortal	immortalize	immortal	
rewarded rewarding	reward	reward		

7

WORD-FORM PRACTICE *Insert the correct form of the italicized word in the blank space.*

1. *invention* Thomas Edison was a famous inventor.

2. *invention* He invented the electric light and the phonograph.

3. *child* "Don't behave so childishly the mother said to her teenage daughter.

4. *arrest* The police arrested Louis for carrying a gun.

5. *invite* He received an invitation from King Oliver.

6. *record* Louis recorded many songs with his jazz band.

7. *record* These records helped make him famous.

8. *blend* His mannerisms were a blend of natural good humor and serious showmanship.

9. *immortal* Louis was a jazz immortal.

10. *child* The boy behaved in a childish manner.

11. *personal* The store personalized my wallet by printing my initials on it.

12. *arrest* The officers made an arrest.

13. *reward* He won the English contest and received a reward.

14. *immortal* Louis achieved immortality.

15. *blend* A martini is a blend of gin and vermouth.

16. *glow* The cigarette glows in the dark.

8 PARTICIPLES   *Insert the correct form of the participle in the blank space.*

1. *immortalize* _____ by his music, Louis will be long remembered.

2. *arrest* The _____ officer took Louis to court.

3. *arrest* The _____ youth was Louis Armstrong.

4. *invite* Only the _____ guests could attend.

5. *invite* The girl gave him an _____ smile.

6. *record*   The _____ artists popularized several songs.

7. *record*   The _____ songs of Louis Armstrong were a sensation.

8. *blend*   The _____ voices of the choir sounded beautiful.

9. *glow*   Louis had a _____ smile.

10. *reward*   Knowing Louis was a _____ experience.

9 READING COMPREHENSION   *Circle the answer (a, b, c, or d) that completes each sentence correctly.*

1. Louis was born in
   a. Chicago.
   b. Kansas City.
   c. New York.
   d. New Orleans.

2. As a kid, Louis lived in
   a. a middle-class neighborhood.
   b. a run-down part of town.
   c. the suburbs.
   d. an expensive apartment.

3. Louis's first instrument was the
   a. cornet.
   b. trumpet.
   c. violin.
   d. drums.

4. As a youth, Louis
   a. traveled a lot.
   b. disliked traveling.
   c. wanted to travel but never had the opportunity.
   d. became a world traveler.

5. Louis *first* played a musical instrument
   a. at the Waifs' Home.
   b. with the Hot Five.
   c. in the bars and cabarets of New Orleans.
   d. with King Oliver's band.

6. When Louis was 22, he
   a. was arrested for carrying a gun.
   b. made a hit record.
   c. made a world tour.
   d. was invited to join King Oliver's band.

7. In his youth, Louis
   a. received a good education.
   b. took singing lessons.
   c. had a very hard life.
   d. received help from the church.

8. A popular song that was an early hit for Louis was
   a. "The Star-Spangled Banner."
   b. "My Old Kentucky Home."
   c. The National Anthem.
   d. "Bugle Call Rag."

9. Louis met the king of
   a. Nigeria.
   b. the Congo.
   c. Uganda.
   d. England.

10. Louis's attitude toward life could best be described as
    a. resentful.
    b. discontented.
    c. discouraged.
    d. full of joy.

10 PREPOSITIONS   *Insert the correct preposition in each blank space.*

1. Jazz was a new kind _____ music, _____ America and the world.

2. Jazz was hard _____ the white musicians to learn.

3. _____ the 1920s, there were many jazz musicians.

4. The career _____ Louis Armstrong spans jazz history, _____ its

   beginnings _____ its later developments.

5. Louis combined talent _____ hard work.

6. Louis sold newspapers _____ the streets.

7. He was a loader _____ a coal yard.

8. Louis was born _____ 1900 _____ a poor section of town.

9. He played _____ the riverboats.

10. _____ a few years, he played _____ bars and cabarets.

11 *CONTROLLED COMPOSITION* *Rewrite the selection below. Two ways are provided. Follow the directions in each step.*

Success

¹To succeed, students *work* hard every day. ²They *read* their assignments, *do* their homework, *study* in the library, and *recite* in class. ³When they have a problem, they *discuss* it with the teacher. ⁴If it is a personal problem, they *make* an appointment with the guidance counselor. ⁵If it is a medical problem, they *see* the school nurse.

⁶After school, students *have* fun. ⁷They *relax* by talking to their friends in the cafeteria. ⁸On weekends, they *hike* in the country. ⁹Evenings, they *date* if they want to.

1. Rewrite the passage, inserting modal auxiliaries before each verb in italics. Use words such as *can, should, must, ought to, able to, might,* and *have to.*

2. Sometimes it's fun to give contrary advice. For comic effect, rewrite the passage, making all the modal auxiliaries negative. Unhappily, the student who follows this advice will surely fail. Your first sentence will read:

To succeed, students *shouldn't* work hard every day.

12 *TOPICS FOR WRITING AND DISCUSSION*

1. Louis became a great success in later life, but his early childhood was hard. Apply this lesson to today's youth. Is it better for kids to struggle a little, or should they have it easy from the start? Explain.

2. Describe the life of a famous person from your country.

3. Louis made a mistake in his youth, but it did not spoil his life. Have you ever had a serious problem in your life? Describe the problem and tell what you did about it.

4. Does Louis Armstrong remind you of someone from your country? Tell why.

5. In his travels abroad, Louis was accepted as an unofficial ambassador from the United States. What qualities in the man made him ideal for this job?

13 DICTATION

1. Lucy was a newcomer in school.
2. Her birthplace was Philadelphia.
3. Her great-grandparents had been pioneers in this country.
4. Some of the students in her school were outstanding.
5. Only a few were brilliant.
6. Many of the students had inborn talents.
7. Eventually some of the students would become preeminent.
8. A few people came from the squalid part of town.
9. Their parents had been illiterate.
10. The students absorbed as much knowledge as they could.
11. In music class, they sang duets.
12. Alice could outperform Jack on the piano.
13. Her playing was extraordinary.
14. It was a blend of skill and insight.
15. After graduating, the students toured the country.

Five

CAN THIS MARRIAGE BE SAVED?

The Story of Joan and Greg

Part I: Joan Talks First

In today's world, marriage is subjected to the same stresses as other cultural institutions. Technological change seems to be affecting everything. People want what is new, what is novel, what is exciting. Trade in the old; buy the latest model. Get a new car, get a new television, get the newest computer. A popular song is a hit today, forgotten tomorrow. Change has become a way of life. Without a backward glance, we change jobs, change careers, change where we live. Not surprisingly, we change our marriage partners, too. In the United States, the marriage rate is 10.6 per 1,000 people. The divorce rate is 5.3 per 1,000, one divorce in every two marriages. Of course, this figure does not include unhappy couples. Where society offered stability, instability has become a way of life. And we are hooked.

But some people are fighting back. When their marriage is in trouble, they try to find out what's wrong. One way is to get professional help from a marriage counselor, a person with special training in psychology and family relations. That is what Joan and Greg did.

Their story is divided into three parts. In Part I, Joan gives her side of the problem. In Part II, Greg tells his side. Finally, in Part III, the marriage counselor gives the couple some thoughtful advice.

(*1*) "When I came home last night, after a particularly brutal day at my office, the breakfast dishes were still piled in the sink, and Greg was stretched out comfortably on the sofa reading a book," said Joan, a tall blond, age 28, with a job as a business analyst for a trade association.

Having lost his job, Greg stayed home and cleaned the house.

"Without raising his eyes from the book, Greg grunted hello. We haven't been married for one year yet, but I might as well be a piece of furniture, the way he ignores me. I wanted to scream or hit him over the head. But I choked back my feelings and forced a smile, which of course he didn't see.

(2)   "We live in Washington, D.C., the nation's capital. For seven months now, Greg has been out of work. He was fired from his job as a congressional aide in the Capitol Building after a fight with his boss. Since then, Greg has spent all his time reading books, solving chess problems and watching television. He has not once looked for a new job. The problem is not so much that I'm working and supporting us. It's his 'don't care' attitude, as though his joblessness should be as unimportant to me as it plainly is to him. If he *really* loved me, he would at least try to carry his share of the load.

(3)   "He says he wants to write a book on politics, which is why he has to read so much. But I think the book is just an excuse to avoid looking for a job and to shut me out of his life. He brings a book to bed every night, and it's been months since we had sex. I think he wishes he had remained a bachelor. Sometimes, I wish he had, too.

(4)   "Actually, I was amazed in the first place that Greg was attracted to me. My mother always predicted that a thin girl like me would never get married. From kindergarten through college, I was always the tallest and homeliest in any group and was avoided by my classmates.

Before leaving for work, Joan glanced at her watch. What do you think she's going to tell Greg?

(5) "The fact that I was a <u>bookworm</u> and always got good marks didn't help. The other kids called me 'Teacher's Pet.' Even my mother seemed ashamed of my scholastic ability. She worried constantly that I had no friends, while my sisters who are little and cute, collected boyfriends by the dozen.

(6) "Before Greg, I had only one boyfriend, a medical student, who almost ruined my life. We dated for five years and planned to get married as soon as he graduated. Since we were engaged, I helped pay his tuition. But the week he got his internship, <u>he eloped with a nurse</u>, sending me a telegram to let me know.

(7) "I was shocked and heartbroken. I lost faith in men, all men, and, worse still, in my <u>own judgment</u>. I gave up all hope of getting married and having children. I decided to forget marriage and concentrate on my career.

(8) "A year later, I met Greg at a professional meeting. When he asked me for a date, I told him frankly that I wasn't in the market for romance, and I explained why. He said I was foolish to judge all men by one <u>heel</u>. He told me that I needed to have a little fun with a great guy—him. One afternoon, he suggested that we leave the conference and take a walk in the park. Well, I went.

(9) "While we were in the park he told me I had a magnificent walk—that I stood tall and looked like a queen. He was proud to be at my side. When I said I was too tall, he said that he was taller. He then said that I reminded him of a poem by Lord Byron, the famous English poet. This poem is about a woman who 'walks in beauty, like the night.'

(10) "I was touched by the quotation, and have treasured it ever since. However, I didn't fall in love right away. Nor did he.

(11) "We got acquainted slowly, over a period of months. Much of our talk was about work. His boss at the time was a hot-tempered politician who liked

Before they were married, Joan and Greg walked hand–in–hand in the park.

to be flattered more than Greg wanted to do. And I had—and still have—a boss who likes to bawl me out for nothing. Greg would give me moral support and raise my ego.

(*12*) "When Greg asked me to marry him, I said yes immediately. I felt a new chapter in my life was beginning, especially when we began talking about having a baby. Although my career had been all-important to me, I decided that if we had a family, I would quit work for a couple of years. Greg liked the idea.

(*13*) "Of course, that hopeful plan came to nothing. Four months after our wedding, Greg was out of a job. It was his own fault. He was fired because of a ridiculous argument with his boss, whom he called an idiot—a stupid idiot, at that. Greg insists he was right. Maybe Greg was right in principle, but in fact *he* was the idiot.

(*14*) "His ex-boss has connections all over the city. When Greg insulted his boss, he walked off without a recommendation. Nothing he could say or do would persuade his ex-boss to rehire him. But I think, despite the guy's huge ego, he has a basic sense of justice. He must realize that Greg did outstanding work for him. Anyhow, I believe he would make a few phone calls for Greg and recommend him for a decent job—*if* Greg would apologize.

(*15*) "With unemployment so high, Greg needs every scrap of influence he can get. But Greg flatly refuses to give in. He's so proud! Whenever I suggest he just call his ex-boss or send him a short note, Greg won't listen. I've even offered to write a note for him, but I get no reaction. He simply stops listening. I can feel him shutting me out, and it breaks my heart, although I don't tell him so. I have a little pride myself.

(*16*)   "These days, he ignores all my suggestions, important or trivial. If I say, 'Let's go to the movies,' he tells me he has to finish a chapter of that nonexistent book, or work on a chess problem in his mind. One night, he made me so mad I knocked over his chess board, scattering the chess pieces in all directions. He just smiled, and that made me madder.

(*17*)   "I'm afraid that I'm turning into a witch like my mother-in-law, who is constantly belittling Greg. No matter what he does, it's never good enough. She clearly favors Greg's sister, who is a lawyer. That mother and daughter are two of a kind—both hypercritical and nagging. Greg has a somewhat gentler disposition. He says he takes after his father, who died when he was young. Greg doesn't seem to mind his mother's insults. Unlike me, Greg is protected against insults.

(*18*)   "Recently I've been feeling hurt a lot. Often, as I wash our dishes in

Greg had held an important job. He was a congressional aide in the Capitol Building, Washington, D.C.

bitchy = persona
r' pelea.

the evening after a bad day with my boss and a cold reception from Greg, I cry out of sheer frustration. I close the door so Greg won't see me.

(*19*)   "When I'm feeling depressed like that, I wonder why Greg married me. I start believing he never loved me. My memories of our courtship seem unreal, as if it were a con game Greg lured me into for selfish reasons. Maybe what he wanted wasn't a wife but a slave who would support him and cook and clean, too.

(*20*)   "Once I was abandoned by a guy for another woman. That won't happen with Greg, I'm sure. But he *has* abandoned me emotionally. In a very real sense, I have no husband. Every day that passes, I live alone."

Exercises

1

SCANNING   *To do this exercise, glance at the text for information, then, eyes up, give the response.*

1. What kind of a day did Joan have at the office?
2. What did she find when she got home?
3. How old is Joan?
4. What kind of work does Joan do?
5. How long have Joan and Greg been married?
6. How did Greg respond when greeted by Joan?
7. What did Joan want to do?
8. Where do Joan and Greg live?
9. How long has Greg been out of work?
10. What was his job before he got fired?
11. Since being fired, what does Greg do all day?
12. How often has he looked for a new job?
13. Who is supporting them?
14. What kind of attitude does Greg have?
15. What would he do if he really loved Joan?
16. What does Greg want to do?
17. Does Joan believe in this ambition?
18. What does Greg bring to bed every night?
19. How has this affected their married life?
20. Who wishes he or she had remained a bachelor?
21. What had Joan's mother predicted?

22. Who was the tallest and homeliest girl in the group?
23. Who was a bookworm?
24. What did the other kids call Joan?
25. Who was ashamed of Joan's scholastic ability?

2 *VOCABULARY DEVELOPMENT* *Study the following words. The paragraph from which each word comes is numbered. After studying these words, do exercise 3.*

fired (*2*)	**homely** (*4*)	**to elope** (*6*)
jobless (*2*)	**date** (*6*)	**to flatter** (*11*)
bachelor (*3*)	**tuition** (*6*)	**to insult** (*14*)
		recommendation (*14*)

1. To be **fired** is to lose one's job, be dismissed.
2. A person without work is **jobless.**
3. A **bachelor** is a single, unmarried person. (man)
4. A **homely** person is plain and unattractive.
5. A **date** is a meeting between persons of the opposite sex interested in each other.
6. **Tuition** is the cost charged by a school for taking classes.
7. To **elope** means to run off and get married secretly.
8. To **flatter** someone is to praise or compliment the person, often insincerely. [Flatery]
9. To **insult** is to offend or abuse someone; treat with contempt.
10. A **recommendation** is a statement, often a letter, presenting someone looking for a job in a favorable light.

3 *VOCABULARY PRACTICE* *Fill in the blank spaces, using the vocabulary words above. Choose words with meanings suggested by the words in parentheses.*

1. Greg and Joan (*were married secretly*) __eloped.__
2. Joan was (*plain, not pretty*) __homely__
3. Joan paid her boyfriend's (*school fees*) __tuition__
4. Greg was (*let go*) __fired__ by his boss.

5. His ex-boss would not write a (*employment letter*) _recommendation_ for Greg.

6. Greg's boss liked to be (*complimented insincerely*) _Flattered_.

7. Greg is (*without work*) _Jobless_

8. Greg and Joan began to (*meet*) _date_ regularly.

9. Joan began to wish Greg had remained a (*single person*) _bachelor_

10. Greg (*spoke rudely to*) _Insulted_ his boss.

④ SYNONYMS   *In the following sentences, replace the italicized word or phrase with the best synonym from the list. Do not use any synonym more than once.*

fired	trivial	grunted
letter of recommendation	piled	capital
courtship	chess	jobless
bachelor	abandoned	insults
heel	sheer	"don't care"
treasured		scrap (pedacitos)

1. The dishes were (*stacked*) _piled_ in the kitchen sink.

2. Greg needs every (*small amount*) _scrap_ of help he can get.

3. Greg didn't mind his mother's (*unpleasant criticisms*) _Insults_

4. Greg's boss (*discharged*) _fired_ him.

5. Joan sometimes cried out of (*pure, unmixed*) _sheer_ frustration.

6. Betty's husband deserted her. He's a real (*unpleasant person*) _heel_.

7. Greg liked to play (*a game*) _chess_.

8. Greg quoted poetry, and Joan (*cherished*) _treasured_ it for months. (Valorar)

9. To help find another job, Greg requested a (*statement of work skills*) _letter of recomendation_ from his boss.

[abendon?]
[abandoned]

10. Greg had (*left*) _abandon_ Joan emotionally.

11. Greg had a (*indifferent*) "_don't care_" attitude.

12. Joan remembered their (*dating period*) _cour_ with pleasure. — *sonido*

courtship

13. Greeting Joan, Greg (*made an animallike sound*) _grunted_ hello.

14. Greg wished he'd remained a (*single person*) _bachelor_

15. Some of her suggestions were (*unimportant*) _trivial_.

5 WORD-FORM CHART   *Study the following words.*

PARTICIPLE	NOUN	VERB	ADJECTIVE	ADVERB
	politics		political	politically
amazing	amazement	amaze		
	prediction	predict	predictable	predictably
	shame	shame	shameful shameless	shamefully shamelessly
engaged	engagement	engage		
eloped	elopement	elope		
	suggestion	suggest	suggestible	suggestibly
	pride		proud	proudly
acquainted	acquaintance	acquaint		
flattered	flattery	flatter		
	hope	hope	hopeful	hopefully
	argument	argue	arguable	arguably

concern

write on paper

6 **WORD-FORM PRACTICE**   *In the blank space, write the correct form of the italicized word.*

1. *hope*   John had a ___hopeful___ attitude.

2. *flatter*   "I hate ___flattery___," the girl said.

3. *engage*   Do you believe in long or short ___engagement___?

4. *shame*   When he's drinking, his behavior is ___shameful___

5. *suggest*   Do you have any ___suggestions___

6. *elopement*   One night Bob and Betty ___eloped___ without telling anyone.

7. *prediction* Her behavior is not very ___predictable___

8. *acquaint*   Is this man an ___acquaintance___ of yours?

9. *pride*   The woman was too ___proud___ for her own good.

10. *argue*   The married couple had their first serious ___argument___ yesterday.

11. *hopeful*   I ___hope___ he's there.

12. *argue*   The truth of that statement is ___arguable___.

13. *amazement* Her intelligence ___amaze___ everyone.

14. *predictable* Your weather ___prediction___ was correct.

15. *politics*   There is always a lot of ___political___ activity at election time.

7 **SYNONYMS**   *Rewrite the following sentences, replacing the word or phrase in italics with the best synonym from the list. Do not use any synonym more than once.*

assistant	intern	pretty
scattered	single man	prefers

constant reader	very hard	emotionally affected
plainest	a poor reason	lying
feeling of self-importance	former	school fees
	foolish	useful friends
		honestly

1. Joan had a _brutal_ day at the office. *very hard*
2. Greg was _stretched out_ on the sofa. *lying*
3. Greg had been a congressional _aide_. *assistant*
4. Writing a book was _an excuse_ to avoid looking for a job. *a poor reason*
5. Joan was a _bookworm_. *constant reader*
6. Joan was the tallest and _homeliest_ girl in her group. *plainest*
7. She paid her boyfriend's _tuition_. *school fees*
8. Joan was _touched_ by the poem. *emotionally affected*
9. Greg's ex-boss had _connections_ all over the city. *useful friends*
10. His boss has a huge _ego_. *feeling of self-importance*
11. Greg's mother _favors_ his sisters. *prefers*
12. Joan's sisters were little and _cute_. *pretty*
13. Joan spoke _frankly_ to Greg. *honestly*
14. Greg had a _ridiculous_ fight with his boss. *foolish*
15. Should Greg call his _ex_-boss? *former*

8 READING COMPREHENSION *On the basis of the story, mark each of the following sentences T if it is true or F if it is false.*

1. _F_ Both Greg and Joan have good jobs.

2. _F_ The couple lives in New York.

3. _T_ Greg had had a fight with his boss.

4. _F_ Joan liked to play chess.

5. _F_ Greg had published a successful book on politics.

6. _F_ Greg was actively looking for a job.

7. _F_ Before Greg, Joan had had several boyfriends.

8. _T_ Joan had helped put her boyfriend through school.

9. _F_ Joan's first boyfriend eloped with his secretary.

10. _F_ Joan met Greg at school.

11. _F_ Almost immediately, Joan felt she knew Greg well.

12. _F_ Although she had a job when they met, Joan placed little emphasis on her career.

13. _T_ Sometimes Joan's boss bawled her out for nothing.

14. _T_ Greg helped to raise Joan's ego.

15. _T_ Greg's mother belittled him constantly.

9 LANGUAGE GAME   *For review practice, play one of the games in the appendix.*

10 SKIT   *Divide the class into groups. Ask each group to invent a marriage problem involving a couple like Joan and Greg. This problem might concern an interfering in-law, a jealous wife or husband, or trouble at work. The group should invent enough characters to give each member a part. Be sure the skit dialogue includes new words and phrases (which the teacher might list on the board), such as* frustrated, fired, pile of dishes in the sink, jobless, letter of recommendation, ex-boss, heel, *and the like.*

After each skit, have the class discuss ways to resolve the problem.

11 CONTROLLED COMPOSITION   *Rewrite the selection below. Two ways are provided. Follow the directions in each step.*

Modeling

[1]Betty is a model. [2]In school, she studied makeup and hairdressing, and had dance training. [3]Today she earns $65 an hour modeling designer dresses. [4]Besides dresses, she also shows fashion luggage and sells cosmetics and jewelry. [5]Betty appears at business conventions and professional meetings. [6]She specializes in showroom modeling. [7]Her work takes her all over the world. [8]She visits Colombia, Turkey, Mexico, Nigeria, and Greece. [9]To keep her figure, she swims, jogs, and works out in a gym. [10]She is one of the most popular models anywhere.

1. Rewrite the selection in the future tense, changing the word "Today," in sentence 3, to "In the future." Begin as follows:

   > Betty is a model. In school she studied makeup and hairdressing, and had dance training. In the future she will earn $65 an hour modeling designer dresses.

2. Rewrite the selection in the present-perfect tense, changing the word "Today," in sentence 3, to "In the past" and using "has" in front of each principal verb. Begin as follows:

   > Betty is a model. In school she studied makeup and hairdressing, and had dance training. In the past, she has earned $65 an hour modeling designer dresses.

12 TOPICS FOR WRITING AND DISCUSSION

1. In the United States, the marriage rate is 10.6 per 1,000 people. The divorce rate is 5.3 per 1,000. That is, one marriage in every two fails. In your opinion, what causes this problem? More particularly, what can Americans do about it?
2. Pretend you are the marriage counselor. What advice would you give Joan to help save her marriage?
3. Discuss a marriage problem with which you are familiar.
4. Describe your idea of a perfect marriage.

13 DICTATION

1. Joan is a business analyst.
2. She is mad at Greg.
3. He left the breakfast dishes in the sink.
4. The couple lives in Washington, D.C.
5. Greg had been a congressional aide.
6. Greg is writing a book on politics.
7. As a kid, Joan was a bookworm.
8. The other kids called her "Teacher's Pet."
9. Greg had a fight with his boss.
10. Joan felt depressed.

Six

CAN THIS MARRIAGE BE SAVED?

Part II: Greg's Turn to Talk

(1)   "I'm well aware Joan is dissatisfied with the way things are going between us," said Greg, age 30, a handsome, six-foot-plus blond. "But there isn't much I can do about it. I feel like I'm at a dead end personally and professionally.

(2)   "I started doing a lot of reading, with the idea of writing a book, but I'm probably kidding myself. I don't have a publisher and haven't written a word. Also, I haven't even looked for a job. Why bother? Jobs are tough enough to find today and I don't make a good first impression on people. In interviews, I seem too unsure of myself.

(3)   "That's because I've been conditioned since boyhood to see myself as second-rate, especially compared to my sister, Betsy. I failed second grade, as my mother will recall to her dying day, the same year Betsy skipped two grades.

(4)   "Betsy and Mom agree on every issue. They describe themselves as political activists; I call them troublemakers. I split away from them and their notions during the Vietnam war. One weekend back then, Mom and Betsy were demonstrating against the war and I went to a recruiting office and volunteered for the Marines. I was turned down because of asthma. Mom and Betsy were overjoyed at my rejection, which they considered side-splittingly funny. Personally, I was not amused.

(5)   "Like everybody else, I prefer cheers to jeers. I thoroughly enjoyed the job I held on Capitol Hill and the compliments that regularly came my way. One time I steered a tricky piece of legislation through several tough committees

82

Joan gave Greg a lot of chores to do. He must clean the house and do the cooking.

and all the political bigshots were talking about it. I'm sorry I lost the job because of a silly argument with my boss. I realize I made a big mistake. However, this doesn't mean I intend to eat dirt and apologize to that guy, regardless of Joan's unsubtle hints.

(6) "Joan's advice and attitude annoy me no end. I was first attracted to her by her graceful walk; now, however, she drags in like the weight of the world is on her shoulders. She glances around the apartment and then gives me a look that makes me feel like a worm. I know at once I should have vacuumed or started supper. It's all in the look. Unfortunately, the day has slipped away so fast I haven't done the chores she considers necessary. She wants to complain about my laziness but is determined to be tactful. I detest tact. It seems like hypocrisy to me.

(7) "Joan used to be straightforward and honest. The first time we met she told me all about a no-good guy who ditched her—the kind of humiliation I would certainly keep to myself. I was flattered by the confidence she put in me and was charmed by her frankness.

(8) "Nowadays, though, she's roundabout in her talk. At times, she sounds like Mom and Betsy needling me in some underhanded fashion. For instance, Joan says she's worried I might get lonesome sitting in the apartment all day. What she means is I should go out and find a job.

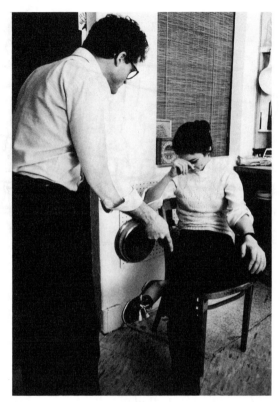

What do you think Greg is saying to Joan?

(9) "Joan knows that I don't get lonesome. I can sit and read or work on a chess problem for hours, even for days, without getting bored. As a kid, I would try to slip away from the supper table to escape Mom and my sister and their endless arguments. My father died when I was young, but even when he was alive he never stuck up for me against my mother. So I had to train myself to shut my ears and be deaf to her and my sister.

(10) "Now I use that 'go deaf' technique on Joan, too. I guess in a way I'm pushing her out of my life. But I just feel too preoccupied to be close to anyone. Although we haven't had sex in months, it doesn't bother me. I have other things on my mind.

(11) "I don't understand why Joan is so upset that I'm out of a job. If *she* weren't making money, *I* would be glad to support both of us. In fact, we once talked about her stopping work to have a baby, and I expected to carry the financial load.

(12) "Frankly, I'm very disappointed that she's not more understanding. After all, *I'm* the one who was fired."

Greg worked for a Congressman helping to prepare legislation. Which Congressman in this picture do you think Greg worked for? Explain why you think so.

Exercises

1 **SCANNING**   *To do this exercise, glance at the text for information, then, eyes up, give the response.*

1. Who is dissatisfied with Greg?
2. How old is Greg?
3. How tall is Greg?
4. Who feels he is at a dead end?
5. What did Greg want to write?
6. Who's kidding himself?
7. How much had Greg written?
8. What are tough to find today?

9. Who doesn't make a good first impression?
10. Who seems unsure of himself?
11. How long has Greg seen himself as second-rate?
12. Which grade did Greg fail?
13. Who will recall this event?
14. How many grades did Betsy skip?
15. What do Betsy and Mom agree on?
16. How do they describe themselves?
17. When did Greg split away from them?
18. What did Greg volunteer for?
19. Why was Greg turned down?
20. Who were overjoyed at his rejection?
21. Who prefers cheers to jeers?
22. What did Greg enjoy on Capitol Hill?
23. What did Greg steer through several committees?
24. Why did Greg lose his job?
25. What did Greg make?

2
VOCABULARY DEVELOPMENT *Study the following words. The paragraph from which each word comes is numbered. After studying these words, do exercise 3.*

publisher (2)	**recruiting officer** (4)	**annoy** (6)
impression (2)	**rejection** (4)	**humiliation** (7)
interview (2)	**political bigshots** (5)	**lonesome** (9)
	Capitol Hill (5)	

1. A **publisher** is a person or a company that prints books, newspapers, or magazines.
2. An **impression** is a mental effect produced by a person or thing. "My first **impression** of Betty was favorable."
3. An **interview** is a meeting to obtain information. "The reporter had an **interview** with the movie star."
4. **Recruitment** is the process by which an organization, such as the armed forces, secures additional personnel. Thus, a **recruiting officer** interviewed Greg about joining the Marines.
5. A **rejection** is a refusal. To **reject** is to discard, get rid of.
6. A **bigshot** is slang for "important person." "The political **bigshots** influenced the government."

7. **Capitol Hill** is the location in Washington, D.C., of the Capitol Building, where the U.S. Congress meets.

8. To **annoy** is to bother or irritate someone.

9. **Humiliation** is the state of being embarrassed, losing dignity and self-respect.

10. To be **lonesome** is to feel depressed or sad due to lack of friends.

3 VOCABULARY PRACTICE *Fill in the blank spaces, using the vocabulary words above.*

1. He liked Sue the first time he saw her. She made a favorable _impression_.

2. Betty decided to join the Air Force. She was interviewed by a _Recruitment office_.

3. The _political big shots_ have too much influence on Capitol Hill.

4. Betty disliked her husband's habits. They really _annoy_ her.

5. When Judy went on vacation, she left her friends at home. For a while afterward, she felt _lonesome_.

6. Sue refused to marry Bill. This _Humiliation rejection_ made him unhappy.

7. I want to talk to this athlete. Can you arrange an _Interview_?

8. Congress meets in the Capitol Building on _Capitol Hill_.

9. To sell a book, you need a _publisher_.

10. Not passing the second grade embarrassed Greg. This _Humiliation_ affected his work for years.

4 VOCABULARY *Circle the letter (a, b, or c) in front of the answer that has the same meaning as the italicized word in the sentence.*

1. Greg felt he was at a *dead end* professionally.
   a. had average opportunities
   b. had good opportunities
   c. had no opportunities

2. In height, Greg was *six feet plus*.
   a. less than six feet
   b. just six feet
   c. more than six feet

3. Greg was turned down by the Marines because of *asthma*.
   a. respiratory condition
   b. high blood pressure
   c. flat feet

4. Greg was *turned down* by the Marines because of asthma.
   a. rejected
   b. accepted
   c. referred elsewhere

5. Greg *steered* a tricky piece of legislation through some tough committees.
   a. guided
   b. blocked
   c. originated

6. Greg did not do the *chores* around the house.
   a. games
   b. small jobs
   c. entertainment

7. Greg's mother and sister *needled* him all the time.
   a. sewed his clothing
   b. made cutting little remarks
   c. helped him at work

8. He should have *vacuumed* the apartment.
   a. cleaned the rugs with a machine
   b. done the dishes
   c. put away the clothes

9. Joan made some *unsubtle* hints about Greg getting a job.
   a. pretty obvious
   b. delicate
   c. hidden

10. Betty used *tact* when handling social situations.
   a. displayed no sense of what to do and say
   b. displayed a poor sense of what to do and say
   c. displayed a good sense of what to do and say

11. Greg disliked *hypocrisy*.
  a. insincere attitudes
  b. wit
  c. beauty

5 WORD-FORM CHART   *Study the following words.*

PARTICIPLE	NOUN	VERB	ADJECTIVE	ADVERB
	person		personal	personally
	profession		professional	professionally
	impression	impress	impressionable	impressionably
	interview interviewer	interview		
	agreement	agree	agreeable	agreeably
	tact		tactful tactless	tactfully tactlessly
	finance	finance	financial	financially
humiliating	humiliation	humiliate		
	apology	apologize	apologetic	apologetically
	understanding	understand	understandable	understandably
	confidence	confide	confidential	confidentially

6 WORD-FORM PRACTICE   *In the blank space, write the correct form of the italicized word.*

1. *finance*   Will you make the _____ arrangements?

2. *apology*   When you offend someone, you should _____.

3. *agreement* Betty is a very _____ person.

4. *tactful* In a difficult social situation, always use _____.

5. *confide* I appreciate your _____.

6. *impression* Children are sometimes quite _____.

7. *profession* The doctor gave his _____ opinion.

8. *person* Don't take the remark _____.

9. *financial* Can you _____ this deal?

10. *interview* The _____ asked a lot of questions.

11. *professional* Engineering is a very good _____.

12. *understand* José's English is clear and _____.

13. *interview* The sports announcer _____ the athlete.

14. *tact* Handle the matter _____.

15. *humiliate* The remarks of his ex-boss added to his _____.

⑦ **VOCABULARY** *From the list below, select the word that best completes each sentence and write it in the blank space. Do not use any word more than once.*

compliments	frankness	dying day
hints	kidding	asthma
failed	volunteer	interview
lonesome	idiot	dissatisfied

1. When people join the army, they _____ their services.

2. A person without friends can feel pretty _____ at times.

3. When Greg did good work, he liked praise and _____.

4. It would have been bad enough if Greg had called his boss a fool. Instead, Greg called him an _____.

5. Joan made indirect suggestions to Greg that he should apologize. Greg did not like these _____.

6. Joan always told Greg the truth. He was charmed by her _____.

7. Greg did not pass a grade level in elementary school. In other words, he _____ that grade.

8. Greg had difficulty breathing. This condition is called _____.

9. Greg wasn't really honest about writing the book. He was only _____ himself.

10. When looking for a job, your first meeting with an employer is called a job _____.

(8) **READING COMPREHENSION** *Choose the wording (a, b, or c) that best completes each sentence. Then rewrite the complete sentence correctly.*

1. Since boyhood, Greg was conditioned to see himself as a
  a. second-rate student.
  b. brilliant student.
  c. high achiever.

2. Greg's sister and mother were
  a. political activists.
  b. political conservatives.
  c. inactive politically.

3. Mom and Betsy thought Greg's rejection by the Marines was
  a. embarrassing.
  b. side-splittingly funny.
  c. incomprehensible.

4. Though Greg was at fault in the disagreement with his boss, he refused to
   a. send flowers.
   b. "eat dirt" and apologize.
   c. take his wife to the movies.

5. It would help Joan if Greg
   a. played 4 games of chess.
   b. did research on his book.
   c. vacuumed the apartment.

6. Greg was first attracted to Joan by her
   a. graceful walk.
   b. attractive figure.
   c. witty conversation.

7. When Joan got home she gave Greg a look that made him feel
   a. like a worm.   *so parte familiar*
   b. terrific.
   c. glad to be alive.

8. When Greg was young, his father
   a. never stuck up for him.
   b. helped him.
   c. gave him money.

9. To escape unpleasant arguments with his family, Greg trained himself to
   a. play chess.
   b. "go deaf." —▷ *No oir los regaños*
   c. write a book.

10. Joan thought her first boyfriend was
    a. a no-good guy.
    b. a desirable date.
    c. God's gift to women.

9 CONTROLLED COMPOSITION   *Rewrite the selection below. Two ways are provided. Follow the directions in each step.*

The Elephant

[1]The elephant is an animal of ancient descent. [2]Amazingly, its ancestors were small creatures without a trunk or tusks. [3]Today, there are only two surviving species: the Asiatic elephant, which lives in India and Sri Lanka, and the African elephant.

⁴The elephant from India is the most familiar. ⁵It rarely exceeds 10 feet in height at the shoulder. ⁶It has small ears and tusks of ivory, and only one "finger" at the tip of the trunk. ⁷The elephant from Africa is usually a little larger. ⁸It has longer tusks, much larger ears, and two "trunk fingers."

⁹The elephant loves the forest, and is especially fond of country in the mountains. ¹⁰The elephant delights in water, and often visits a river or lake for a drink or a bath.

¹¹The elephant lives as long as a hundred years. ¹²It is considered the most intelligent of all animals. ¹³Perhaps that is why the elephant lives a life of such peace and contentment.

1. Rewrite the selection, changing the following phrases found after nouns to single-word modifiers. Place the words before the nouns they modify: *from India* (sentence 4), *of ivory* (sentence 6), *from Africa* (sentence 7), *in the mountains* (sentence 9), *of peace and contentment* (sentence 13). Remember, when a word is moved around in a sentence, changed from a noun to an adjective, you may also have to change its word form, as follows:

Noun	Adjective
India	Indian
Africa	African
mountains	mountainous
peace	peaceful
contentment	contented

2. Rewrite the passage. Change *the elephant* (sentence 1) to *elephants,* and make all other necessary changes in the passage. Your first sentence will say:

> Elephants are animals of ancient descent.

10 TOPICS FOR WRITING AND DISCUSSION

1. When a marriage is in trouble, what is the best way to save it? Should the couple attempt to solve their own problems? Should they go for help to a relative (the wife's mother, for instance)? Should they consult a religious authority, perhaps a minister, priest, or rabbi? Or should they go to an outsider, such as a marriage counselor? Which "expert" would give the most reliable advice? Tell why you think so.

2. Compare Greg's version of the marriage with Joan's. Can you find dif-

ferences in their stories that throw light on the problem? Who do you think is most at fault? Tell why you think so.

3. Pretend you are the marriage counselor. What advice would you give Greg?

4. How would a problem of this kind be solved in your country? Explain the advantages of your system.

Seven

CAN THIS MARRIAGE BE SAVED?

Part III: The Counselor Speaks

(1) "Joan and Greg were locked in a no-win struggle," said the counselor. "Joan was shattered when Greg began to depend on her so heavily after he lost his job. She felt he was taking advantage of her, just as the medical student had used her. Greg, on the other hand, thought of himself as having lost not only his job, but stature in the eyes of others. With unemployment so high, he felt particularly dejected—a fairly common reaction these days among those out of work. He thought Joan should show him more sympathy. Unfortunately, they weren't able to express their feelings to each other.

(2) "Joan supposed that Greg was strong in the areas where she was weak. She thought he was unaffected by his mother's insults, and was oblivious to her own fading confidence in him. But she was wrong. As a child, Greg had developed severe insecurities that derived from his mother's criticism. The fact that he didn't have a father added to his lonely feelings. His success at his Capitol Hill job had greatly boosted his self-esteem. But when he was fired, Greg's old self-doubts took charge.

(3) "While Greg tried, sometimes unsuccessfully, to hide his insecurities, Joan kept her self-doubts on the surface. As a child, Joan regarded herself as inferior to her 'cute, little' sisters. She learned to downgrade her assets and emphasize her shortcomings with the hope of being contradicted by others and thus reassured. This tiresome 'poor me' technique was effective with Greg in the beginning. So long as he held his job on Capitol Hill with a salary higher than

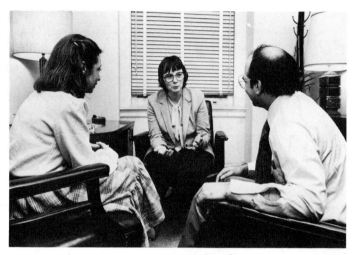

A married couple in trouble can sometimes get help from a marriage counselor.

hers, he was glad to scoff at Joan's self-doubts. He told her she was beautiful and desirable.

(4) "But when Greg lost his job and began feeling sorry for himself, he wasn't about to praise Joan. Instead, he withdrew into his private world, and Joan became increasingly desperate. And no wonder. She was deprived of sex, cooperation around the house, and her husband's companionship. If she offered a suggestion, he tuned her out, as he had done with his mother.

(5) "Joan had been a sacrificial victim—a self-chosen role—long enough. I told her that if she wanted her empty marriage to change, she must risk losing it. She must demand that Greg agree to some of her wishes. She must tell him to shape up or ship out.

(6) "When Greg indignantly refused to participate in group therapy, which was Joan's first demand, she told him she would move out of the apartment. He got the message and entered group therapy.

(7) "Joan and Greg were placed in separate groups with people bothered by problems similar to their own. Within the group, they began talking openly. Joan learned from other members of her group to be less passive, not to accept unfair burdens that others, including her husband and boss, might put on her. Greg found that other men in the group were unemployed and not ashamed to admit it. They were astonished at his refusal to apologize to his boss—and told him that he was a fool.

(8) "Greg took advice, almost for the first time in his life. He wrote a letter of apology to his boss and asked for help in finding a job. The politician not only accepted the apology but made several phone calls. Within a few weeks, Greg had found a job. Although he had to take a pay cut, Greg enjoys the new position, and feels he can be a success.

In group therapy, people sit in a circle and discuss their problems. The members of the group help each other.

Happy again, this couple can make a new start on their marriage.

(9)   "Slowly the misunderstandings between the two are diminishing. Their sexual relationship is improving. Greg has learned to communicate more easily, and Joan has received some of the reassurance she needs from her group, and now requires less from Greg. She no longer thinks he wants to take advantage of her.

(10)   "Both Joan and Greg have stopped regarding themselves as losers and are beginning to understand that each has something worthwhile to offer the other. They are even talking again about starting a family."

Exercises

1 SCANNING   *To do this exercise, glance at the text for information, then, eyes up, give the response.*

1. Who was locked in a no-win struggle?
2. Why was Joan shattered?
3. What did Joan feel?
4. What did Greg think?
5. Why did he feel so dejected?
6. Whom did he think should show more sympathy?
7. What were they unable to express?
8. What did Joan suppose?
9. Whom did she think was unaffected by insults?
10. Who was wrong?
11. What had Greg developed as a child?
12. What else added to his lonely feelings?
13. What boosted his self-esteem?
14. Why did Greg's self-doubts reappear?
15. Who kept her self-doubts on the surface?
16. To whom did Joan regard herself as inferior?
17. Who used a tiresome "poor me" technique?
18. Who scoffed at Joan's self-doubts?
19. Why did Greg feel sorry for himself?
20. Where did Greg withdraw?

2 **VOCABULARY DEVELOPMENT** *Study the following words. The paragraph from which each word comes is numbered. After studying these words, do exercise 3.*

counselor *(1)*	**confidence** *(2)*	**desperate** *(4)*
sympathy *(1)*	**insecurity** *(2)*	**victim** *(5)*
oblivious *(2)*	**boost** *(2)*	**group therapy** *(6)*
		passive *(7)*

1. A **counselor** is a person who gives advice on personal or academic problems.
2. **Sympathy** is a feeling of pity and tenderness for others.
3. To be **oblivious** is to be unaware of yourself or your surroundings.
4. **Confidence** is a strong belief in yourself or in others.
5. **Insecurity** is the condition of self-doubt, lack of confidence.
6. To **boost** something is to raise or increase it.
   "She **boosted** his self-confidence."
7. To be **desperate** is to feel that all is lost; be ready to take any risk, regardless of danger.
8. A **victim** is a person or animal suffering injury and/or pain, even death, at the hands of others or from some natural disaster.
   "She was the **victim** of her brother's anger."
9. **Group therapy** involves a circle of people seeking insight into their social/emotional problems through informal discussions.
10. **Passive** means disinterested, inactive, offering no resistance.

3 **VOCABULARY PRACTICE** *Fill in the blank spaces, using the vocabulary words above.*

1. One way to resolve marriage problems is to meet informally with others. This is called _Group therapy_.

2. Another way to solve marriage problems is to seek the advice of a marriage _counselor_.

3. Phyllis believed in herself. She had _confidence_.

4. Jack complimented Betty on her appearance. His compliment __boosted__ her morale considerably.

5. On a hike, Sam and Phyllis ran out of food and water. Their situation was __desperate__

6. Joe was in a daze, completely __oblivious__ to his surroundings.

7. Sally lacked confidence, had self-doubt. She had feelings of __Insecurity__

8. The little dog was injured. We gave it help and __simpathy__

9. The boy offered no resistance, would do nothing for himself. He was com-pletely __passive__

10. Money was collected to help the __victim__ killed in the flood.

4 WORD-FORM CHART   *Study the following words.*

PARTICIPLE	NOUN	VERB	ADJECTIVE	ADVERB
	sympathy	sympathize	sympathetic	sympathetically
	indignation		indignant	indignantly
developing	development	develop	developmental	developmentally
	derivation	derive		
	criticism	criticize	critical	critically
cooperating	cooperation	cooperate	cooperative	cooperatively
	suggestion	suggest	suggestible	
sacrificing	sacrifice	sacrifice	sacrificial	sacrificially
	contradiction	contradict	contradictory	
struggling	struggle	struggle		

5

WORD-FORM PRACTICE   *In the blank space, write the correct form of the italicized word.*

1. *cooperate*   The prisoner was very _____ in jail.

2. *contradiction*   The facts _____ what you are saying.

3. *derive*   What is the _____ of this word?

4. *criticize*   Betty had a _____ attitude.

5. *sympathize*   Please send a _____ card to the sick person.

6. *indignant*   When insulted, she responded _____.

7. *struggle*   The two men _____ for the money.

8. *sacrificial*   I will make any _____ for my country.

9. *suggestion*   She was very _____.

10. *development*   Did he _____ good habits?

11. *indignant*   She showed her _____.

12. *sympathetic*   The mother _____ with her injured child.

13. *cooperate*   We request your _____.

14. *develop*   Personal _____ is important to me.

15. *sacrificial*   Do not _____ accuracy for speed.

6

ANTONYMS   *For each word at the right, find the correct antonym in the list at the left. Write the antonym in the blank space. Do not use any antonym more than once.*

salary increase
medical
pride
reaction

1. _self-doubt_ confidence

2. _inferiority_ superiority

child
strengths
hired
unattractive
public
reduce
self-doubt
inferiority
praise — *hablar bien*
found
active
rejected

Proud - adj) *orgulloso*
Pride - noun)

3. _active_ passive

4. _praise_ insult

5. _found_ lost

6. _rejected_ accepted

7. _reduce_ boost

8. _public_ private

9. _hired_ fired

10. _unattractive_ cute

11. _strengths_ shortcomings

12. _pride_ shame

13. _salary increase_ pay cut

7 SYNONYMS *Rewrite the following sentences, replacing the word or phrase in italics with the best synonym from the list. Do not use any synonym more than once.*

stature   contradicted   position
dejected   oblivious   shattered
hide   salary   derived
companionship unemployed   downgrade
child   money   therapy

1. He gained (*importance*) _stature_ in the eyes of others.

2. Her confidence was (*destroyed*) _shattered_.

3. Greg left (*in low spirits*) _dejected_.

4. His insecurities (*came*) _derived_ from his mother's criticisms.

[*derived*]

5. She tried to (*conceal*) _hide_ her self-doubt.

6. Unfortunately, Joan began to (*de-emphasize*) _downgrade_ her good points.

7. His statements (*were the opposite of*) _contradicted_ hers.

8. Dazed, she was (*unaware*) _oblivious_ of her surroundings.

9. They both took part in group (*treatment*) _therapy_

10. Joan was deprived of her husband's (*friendship*) _companionship_

11. Both received the same (*pay*) _salary_.

12. For a while, Greg was (*out of work*) _unemployed._

13. Now he enjoys his new (*job*) _position_.

8 READING COMPREHENSION *On the basis of the story, mark each of the following sentences T if it is true or F if it is false.*

1. _T_ The marriage of Joan and Greg was heading toward a dead end.

2. _F_ After Greg lost his job, Joan enjoyed having him depend on her.

3. _T_ Greg always concealed his insecurities.

4. _F_ Joan felt more intelligent than her sisters and generally superior.

5. _T_ Joan's "poor me" technique worked with Greg in the beginning.

6. _T_ When Greg was employed, he scoffed at Joan's self-doubts.

7. _T_ After being fired, Greg deprived Joan of sex, help with the housework, and companionship.

8. _T_ Both Joan and Greg began group therapy.

9. _F_ Greg refused to send his boss a letter of apology.

10. _T_ By popular standards, this story has a happy ending.

9
SKIT *Divide the class into groups for a skit involving a counselor.*

Have each group make up a marriage problem, with students taking the role of the wife, the husband, and the counselor. Other students can pretend to be relatives of the couple, or their children, even friends or neighbors, until all have parts. Have the wife speak first. Using vocabulary from the reading, the wife should present a specific list of grievances. Then have the husband give his version. The other participants speak next. Finally, have the counselor advise the couple.

After the skit, have the class discuss the problem and evaluate the counselor's advice.

10
GAMES *For review practice, turn to a game in the appendix.*

11
CONTROLLED COMPOSITION *Rewrite the selection below. Two ways are provided. Follow the directions in each step.*

George Washington

[1]George Washington, the first President of the United States, was a busy man and never *out of work*. [2]Being elected President in 1789 *boosted* his morale. [3]Washington loved the *position*. [4]The position gave him much pleasure. [5]This pleasure, he felt, was part of his *salary*.

[6]Washington was almost never *dejected*. [7]He was *sympathetic* toward the poor but popular with all the people. [8]The people elected him twice.

[9]His wife, Martha, could not *hide* her pride in her famous husband. [10]The two of them had many years of marriage and *friendship*. [11]In later years, Washington was much honored. [12]He was called the Father of His Country.

1. Rewrite the selection, substituting synonyms for the words in italics, all of which were studied in this chapter.
2. Rewrite the selection, combining sentences 3 and 4, 7 and 8, and 11 and 12 with words like *who, which,* and *that*. Omit any words made unnecessary by this combination.

12
TOPICS FOR WRITING AND DISCUSSION

1. Is marriage out of date ? Tell why you think it is (or is not) still useful to society.

2. In recent years, some American couples have experimented with alternatives to traditional marriage. They set up communes, where several couples lived together in the same house. In another case, college authorities relaxed the rules on dormitory use, permitting complete access to the building for boys and girls at all hours. In still another case, college-age couples shared expenses by moving into the same apartment, sometimes with their parents' permission. Do you think these experiments have any value? Tell why you think so.

3. Pretend you are a marriage counselor. A young husband and wife tell you they want a divorce. How would you conduct the interview, and what advice would you give the couple?

4. Invent an imaginary marital problem. First tell the husband's side. Then tell the wife's. Finally, explain how this couple can resolve its problems.

5. Do you believe the counselor gave good advice to Joan and Greg? Explain your opinion.

13 DICTATION

1. Greg felt dejected.
2. He had lost stature in the eyes of others.
3. Shouldn't Joan show more sympathy?
4. They couldn't express their feelings.
5. Greg had severe insecurities.
6. His job boosted his self-esteem.
7. Greg withdrew into his private world.
8. Joan became desperate.
9. The couple started group therapy.
10. They don't regard themselves as losers anymore.

Eight

CHOOSING A CAREER

How do you choose a career? Many students finish high school and begin college without a clear idea of what they want to do in life. Part of the problem is the size and complexity of the job market itself. Seven hundred and sixty-three different occupations were listed in a recent publication of the United States Department of Labor, and this list is probably incomplete. With so many kinds of work, how can you tell which will interest you? And what about the job outlook? Some of these occupations are already overcrowded. In old industries, there may be little need for new workers, while new and growing industries will offer good jobs, now and in the future. Finally, how can you make the best use of your own special talents? Those who know themselves often find the best jobs. The article that follows does not answer all these questions, but it does try to get you started.

Part I: Getting Started

(*1*) For most people, choosing a career isn't easy, yet it is one of the most important decisions you will make in your life. Find the right career, and you will be happy and successful. Find the wrong career, and you may be unhappy and unsuccessful. It pays, therefore, to explore your choice of occupation from every angle, collect as much information as you can, actually try different kinds of work before making up your mind. Above all, evaluate yourself. Be sure you know your own interests and talents.

(*2*) Unfortunately, not everyone takes this trouble. Those who don't, can

A civil engineer builds roads and bridges.

make costly mistakes. For example, some people simply follow in the footsteps of a parent or a relative. One young man I know became a doctor because that was his father's profession. Yet he could not stand the sight of blood. Watching an operation made him sick to his stomach. One day he had to amputate a leg, and, after making the first cut, fainted in the operating room. A young woman I know became an accountant although she hated math. Her uncle encouraged her by promising a job in his company. It took her several years, and several disasters with the company books, before she realized her mistake.

(3) Procrastinating, postponing a decision, is another error people make. *Mañana* is the Spanish word for it. I'll get started tomorrow, or next week, or next year. These people refuse to face the problem, hoping it will go away. But if you don't take the first step now, how can you plan for the future, take the right courses in school, get in the right programs? Procrastinators just drift, missing many opportunities.

(4) Well then, how *do* you find a career? Jascha Heifetz was a concert violinist at the age of thirteen. Shirley Temple was a movie star at the age of five. Most of us are not so talented, or so lucky. Everyone has skills, but yours may not be so obvious; may, in fact, go undetected. Your career search has to look for everything. Be systematic. Analyze your problem. Determine what information you have. Then go after the information you need. Here are two methods that may help.

(5) *First,* start with yourself. Make a list or inventory of your interests, your talents, and abilities. Most people have a lot of these, but in the beginning they are undeveloped and may not seem outstanding. By concentrating on a few,

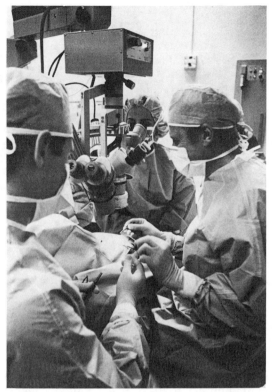

To prevent infection, doctors and nurses wear gowns, caps, and face masks.

or on one, you may surprise yourself, and everyone else, at how good you can get.

(6)   The interest inventory that follows covers the six major fields in which most people find careers: (1) science, (2) the arts, (3) social service, (4) business, (5) sales, (6) mechanical. To find where your interests lie, enter your score in the column at the left: 1 = dislike; 2 = neutral; 3 = like. Then add up your score.

(7)

	Interest Inventory	
Score	*Scientific Career: Useful Skills*	*Useful Personality Traits*
	1. good at math	observant
	2. enjoy studying scientific principles	logical
	3. read tables, graphs, charts	objective
	4. investigate biological and chemical phenomena	systematic
		analytical
	5. enjoy reasoning and making log-ical deductions	inquisitive
		accurate

Score	*Artistic Career: Useful Skills*	*Useful Personality Traits*

Artistic Career: Useful Skills — *Useful Personality Traits*

1. possess special ability in dance, art, or music
2. good body coordination
3. good sense of color
4. good sense of spatial relations
5. value beauty and beautiful things

creative
unconventional
original
sensitive
expressive
reflective

Social-Service Career: Useful Skills

1. like to help people solve their personal problems
2. enjoy community work
3. get satisfaction from assisting elderly, sick, and needy people
4. communicate well
5. enjoy paper work, filing, keeping records

interested in others
understanding
patient
sensitive
sociable
listen well
ethical
helpful

Business Career: Useful Skills

1. interested in manufacturing a product
2. interested in making profits
3. interested in office management
4. type well and accurately
5. file and keep business records

efficient
accurate
cheerful
honest
reliable
discreet
careful
cooperative

Sales Career: Useful Skills

1. enjoy talking to people
2. like to explain and demonstrate products
3. keep good records
4. write sales slips accurately
5. interested in merchandising

persuasive
helpful
enthusiastic
courteous
optimistic
helpful

Mechanical Career: Useful Skills

1. like to work with machines
2. read plans and blueprints
3. good at basic math
4. use formulas
5. make things with my hands

accurate
precise
methodical
deliberate
logical
practical
systematic

(*8*)   After taking the test, add up your scores and write them below: (1) Scientific Career ____; (2) Artistic Career ____; (3) Social Service Career ____; (4) Business Career ____; (5) Sales Career ____; (6) Mechanical Career ____.

(*9*)   A high score indicates great interest. A low score indicates little interest. Do not be surprised if you score well in more than one area. That is normal at this stage. In fact, some careers straddle two fields. For example, a nurse should score high in both science and social service. But you should begin to specialize, to channel your interests toward some specific goal.

(*10*)   There is a *second* way to choose a career: survey the job field.

Action	*Procedure*
1. Begin with an open mind. The career of a parent or a relative may *or may not* be right for you.	Talk to as many different people as possible about their work. Visit them at their jobs to see if this work appeals to you.
2. Determine your interests, abilities, and aptitudes; find out what you do well and what you do less well.	Take aptitude or interest tests, available through your school counselor.
3. Compare a knowledge of yourself—your interests—with the requirements of various kinds of work.	Refer to books and other publications for job descriptions.
4. Determine realistically if you have the academic ability, time, and funds necessary to complete the training required by a specific career.	Talk with teachers. Evaluate your aptitude tests. Look into financial-aid programs.
5. At this point, you may still be interested in several fields. This is normal. Eventually these interests will merge as you discover the work you do best and enjoy most.	Take elementary courses at school in your different fields of interest. Read about successful people in these fields.
6. After choosing a major, work out a program of courses that will lead to your goal. Then pursue your objective with all your energy.	Discuss a program with advisers in your major department, and with the department chairperson. Get some on-the-job experience by assisting a teacher, through a school club, or through part-time employment.

(*11*)   Here is a *partial* list of careers in the six main divisions:

(1) *Scientific Career*

Engineer	Biologist	Chemist
Geologist	Mathematician	Physicist
Meteorologist	Statistician	Science Teacher
Oceanographer	Astronomer	Doctor/Nurse

(2) *Artistic Career*

Actor/Actress	Singer	Interior Designer
Dancer	Architect	
Musician	Commercial Artist	

(3) *Social-Service Career*

Social Worker	Clergy
Recreation Worker	Counselor
Home Economist	

(4) *Business Career*

Accountant	Lawyer
Business Manager	Marketing Expert
Bank Officer	Personnel and Labor-Relations Expert
Credit Manager	Computer Programmer

Professional dancers perform in ballets, operas, and in many other kinds of stage entertainment.

(5) *Sales Career*
Insurance Agent
Manufacturers' Representative
Real-Estate Broker
(6) *Mechanical Career*
Mechanic (automobile, boat, farm equipment, industrial machinery)
Office-Equipment Expert
Air-Conditioning Expert

Part II: Planning a Career—College Programs

(*12*)   Sally and Bill are freshman students at Northern University, talking about their careers.

BILL: "What are you majoring in?"

SALLY: "I'm majoring in Engineering. This is a nontraditional field for women. But more and more women are going into it. When I graduate, there will be a lot of job opportunities with good salaries. It is an interesting field if you're good at math. Fortunately, that's my best subject. What are you majoring in, Bill?"

BILL: "I like math, too. But I'm going to major in Business Administration. My interest is marketing, which is a subdivision of 'Bus Ad.'"

SALLY: "Marketing—that sounds interesting. What kind of work does it involve?"

BILL: "It includes everything—buying and selling, shipping and advertising. Here's the college catalogue. Look at the courses I have to take. In a 4-year program, I need 120 credits to graduate. These are divided into three parts—the General Education requirement, which includes about 40 credits in Humanities and Social Sciences; 28 credits in electives; and 52 credits in my major field. Here are some of my requirements:*

BUS 105   Introduction to Electronic Data Processing, (3 cr.)
BUS 201   Accounting I (3 cr.)
BUS 202   Accounting II (3 cr.)
BUS 220   Marketing Principles (3 cr.)

*Using this material as a point of departure, discuss the academic programs in your school. Explain the course catalogue, and have students look up the requirements for their major fields.

BUS   321   Principles of Advertising (3 cr.)
BUS   420   Marketing Research (3 cr.)

And a lot more besides that. What about you, Sally? What do you have to take?"

SALLY: "In Engineering, I also need 40 credits in General Education, 28 credits in electives, and 54 credits in my field. Here are some of my requirements:

MATH   224   Calculus I (4 cr.)
CSC   211   Introduction to Computer Programming (3 cr.)
PHY   112   General Physics (4 cr.)
PHY   310   Statistics (3 cr.)
CHE   111   Fundamental Principles of Chemistry I (4 cr.)

It's a lot of work. But it's worth it."

BILL: "It certainly is. Can I get you another cup of coffee?"

SALLY: "Yes, Bill. That would be very nice."

A chemist's research creates new products for home and industry.

Four Years Later

(13)   Sally and Bill are again in the cafeteria talking.

SALLY: "Isn't it great about graduation?"

BILL: "Yes, it is. I'm already looking for a job, and have even written my first letter of application. What do you think of it?"

(14)

> 37 Rosedale Road
> Detroit, Michigan 48219
> May 2, 1990
>
> Ms. Doris C. Johnson
> Director of Personnel
> Lone Star Manufacturing Company
> 134 North Street
> New York, New York 10013
>
>
> Dear Ms. Johnson:
>
>
> Mr. William Smith, job counselor at Northern University, informed me that there will be an opening in your sales division on July 1, 1990.
>
> I will graduate from Northern University on June 6, with a major in marketing. I have taken courses in business administration and computer programing, a subject in which I have a particular interest. For the past two summers, I have worked as a student volunteer in the sales division at Hill Industries. At school this year, I was secretary in charge of advertising for the student council. From the job description available to Mr. Smith, I believe that I meet all the requirements of the position.
>
> I would appreciate the opportunity to discuss my qualifications for this job with you at your convenience.
>
> Sincerely,
>
> *Bill Leonard*
>
> Bill Leonard

SALLY: "It looks like a good letter. I hope you get the job."

A teacher's work is interesting, varied, and useful.

Lab technicians analyze blood and urine, and culture bacteria. Their work is indispensable in a modern hospital.

Exercises

1
SCANNING   *To do this exercise, glance at the text for information, then, eyes up, give the response.*

1. What is difficult for most people?
2. What is one of your most important decisions?
3. What happens if you find the right career?
4. What happens if you find the wrong career?
5. What should you explore?
6. What should you collect?
7. What should you try?
8. What should you know?
9. Does everyone take this trouble?
10. What happens to those who don't?

11. What do some people do?
12. What happened to one young man?
13. What did he amputate?
14. Who fainted?
15. What happened to the young woman?
16. What do procrastinators do?
17. Who was Jascha Heifetz?
18. Who was Shirley Temple?
19. Is everyone as talented as they?
20. What should you look for in your career search?
21. Should you be systematic?
22. Should you analyze your problem?
23. What should you determine?
24. What should you go after?
25. In the first method, who do you start with?

2 **VOCABULARY DEVELOPMENT** *Study the following words. The paragraph from which each word comes is numbered. After studying these words, do exercise 3.*

career (*introduction*)	**procrastinator** (*3*)	**goal** (*10*)
talent (*introduction*)	**interest inventory** (*5*)	**Humanities** (*12*)
accountant (*2*)	**personality traits** (*7*)	**electives** (*12*)
		major field (*12*)

1. A **career** is an occupation or lifework. A **profession** usually requires advanced education.
2. A **talent** is a natural aptitude or ability to do something. "That artist is very **talented**."
3. An **accountant** is the person who keeps business records, usually involving financial transactions.
4. A **procrastinator** is someone who puts off, or postpones, till tomorrow what should be done today; that is, he or she **procrastinates.**
5. An **interest inventory** is a list of things you are good at or like to do.
6. **Traits** are distinguishing characteristics. Your personality **traits** are the distinctive qualities that make you a unique person.

7. A **goal** is an aim or object in life.

8. The **Humanities** are one of the major divisions of knowledge, and include liberal-arts subjects, especially literature, history, and philosophy.

9. **Electives** are courses that are not required but are free choices among the offerings of the school.

10. Your **major field** in school is your area of specialization, your chief field of interest.

3 **VOCABULARY PRACTICE** *Fill in the blank spaces, using the vocabulary words above.*

1. Bill habitually puts off all work till tomorrow. He is a _procrastinator_.

2. Sally keeps the books in our office. She is a very good _accountant_.

3. At school this year, I am going to take courses in English, History, and Philosophy. These subjects are given in the _Humanities_ Division.

4. In addition to my required courses, I am also going to take some nonrequired courses, called _Electives_.

5. Before choosing a career, it is a good idea to analyze your skills and talents by making an _interest inventory_.

6. I want to become an Engineer. This is my aim or _goal_ in life.

7. My _personality traits_ are the characteristics that make me different from everyone else.

8. Lois plays the piano. She has a _talent_ for music.

9. My minor field is History. My _major field_ is Engineering.

10. What do you want to do in life? In other words, what are your _career_ goals?

4 ***ADJECTIVES*** *Study the following words.*

observant	unobservant
enthusiastic	unenthusiastic
helpful	unhelpful
original	unoriginal
reflective	unreflective
sociable	unsociable
ethical	unethical
reliable	unreliable
cooperative	uncooperative
systematic	unsystematic
methodical	unmethodical
sensitive	insensitive
efficient	inefficient
accurate	inaccurate
discreet	indiscreet
practical	impractical
patient	impatient
precise	imprecise
honest	dishonest
courteous	discourteous
logical	illogical

IA. *Assign the adjectives for home study.* **IB.** *In the next lesson, pair off students at their seats for adjective practice. Have students take turns giving the cue and making the response in a sentence pattern.*

Example: Student 1 observant
Student 2 Jack is observant. Bill is unobservant.
Student 2 enthusiastic
Student 1 Jack is enthusiastic. Bill is unenthusiastic.

Practice the same-prefix adjectives as a group first. Then mix them up.

II.   *This practice can be turned into a class activity (books closed), with one student giving an adjective, then calling on someone else in the class for the sentence pattern.*

III.   *To continue the lesson, have the class add other skills and traits to the six groups. To help, the teacher might put some examples on the board, then have the class decide which career they fit best.*

IV.   *Another list could be developed of traits to avoid: laziness, discourtesy, rudeness, and so on.*

5 SYNONYMS   *Rewrite the following sentences, replacing the word or phrase in italics with the best synonym from the list. Do not use any synonym more than once.*

undetected	nontraditional	marketing
trivial	survey	drift
amputate	goals	career
skills	errors	electives

1. What *occupation* are you preparing for?   *career*
2. Do you have any special *talents?*   *skills*
3. The doctor had to *cut off* someone's leg.   *amputate*
4. Procrastinators *move aimlessly* from one day to the next.   *drift*
5. Betty's musical talent went *unnoticed* for years.   *undetected*
6. Everyone should *look over* the job field.   *survey (ver)*
7. Do you have any *objectives* in life?   *goals*
8. Being a fire fighter is *new and unusual* work for a woman.   *nontraditional*
9. How many *nonrequired courses* are you taking this semester?   *electives*
10. I don't like to make *mistakes.*   *errors*

6 WORD-FORM CHART   *Study the following words.*

PARTICIPLE	NOUN	VERB	ADJECTIVE	ADVERB
occupied	occupation	occupy		
	decision	decide	decisive	decisively

PARTICIPLE	NOUN	VERB	ADJECTIVE	ADVERB
	success	succeed	successful	successfully
	system	systematize	systematic	systematically
	analysis	analyze	analytic	analytically
developed	development	develop	developmental	
concentrated	concentration	concentrate		
	science		scientific	scientifically
manufactured	manufacturer	manufacture		
	logic		logical	logically
interested interesting	interest	interest		
	efficiency		efficient	efficiently
	persuasion	persuade	persuasive	persuasively
	accuracy		accurate	accurately

7 WORD-FORM PRACTICE   *In the blank space, write the correct form of the italicized word.*

1. *decision*   She could not _decide_ (verb) what to do.

2. *system*   The employees worked _systematically_ (adverb)

3. *analysis*   Chemists _analyze_ (verb) substances.

4. *logical*   Among her courses, she's taking _logic_ (noun) this semester.

5. *occupy*   What is your _occupation_ (noun) ?

6. *success*   He had a very _successful_ (adj) career.

write on paper

7. *manufactured* General Motors is a ___(manufacturer — noun)___ that ___(manufacture — verb)___ automobiles.

8. *interested* Did you ever take an ___(interest — noun)___ inventory?

9. *successful* Don't let ___(successful — adj)___ go to your head.

10. *logic* Please give a ___(logical — adjective)___ explanation.

11. *efficient* Lois always does her work ___(efficiently — adverb)___.

12. *development* Can you ___(develop — verb)___ those ideas further?

13. *interested* Math ___(interests — verb)___ me a lot.

14. *succeed* Is Lois ___(succesful — adjective)___ in business?

15. *persuade* Sally is a very ___(persuasive — adj)___ salesperson.

16. *accuracy* The accountant keeps ___(accurate — adj)___ records.

17. *decide* He is quite ___(diasive — adj)___ when making up his mind.

18. *persuade* She spoke ___(persuasively — adverb)___.

19. *develop* Child psychologists study the ___(development — noun)___ of children.

20. *science* Let's analyze this problem ___(scientifically — adverb)___.

8 **CAREER MATCHING** *In the list at the left, find the word or phrase that best matches the job at the right. Write your choice in the space.* <u>*Do not use a career word more than once.*</u>

labor-relations expert
musician
mechanic
credit manager
nutritionist
civil engineer
lawyer
accountant

1. ___lawyer___ handles legal cases

2. ___civil engineer___ builds roads and bridges

3. ___accountant___ keeps the company books

4. ___Architect___ designs houses and office buildings

real-estate broker
geologist
architect
social worker
clergy
academic counselor
recreation worker
statistician
dance director

5. _academic counselor_ advises students

6. _musician_ plays an instrument in an orchestra

7. _statistician_ analyzes numerical facts and data of all kinds

8. _recreation worker_ organizes sports and games on a playground

9. _social worker_ helps people with family problems

10. _clergy_ responsible for your spiritual life

11. _nutritionist_ plans menus for hospitals and school cafeterias

12. _labor relation expert_ helps settle strikes and other employee/management problems

13. _mechanic_ fixes your car engine

14. _geologist_ studies rock and other earth formations

9 PREPOSITIONS   *Insert the correct preposition in each blank space.*

1. Choosing a career is one _____ your most important decisions.

2. I want a major _____ music with a minor _____ dance.

3. History was one _____ two electives.

4. Counselors employed _____ schools help _____ hard decisions.

5. Most people have a lot _____ skills and a lot _____ talents.

6. Mathematicians sometimes concentrate _____ theoretical problems.

7. The requirement _____ this job is four years _____ college.

8. He received his degree _____ 1985 _____ the sixth _____ June.

9. She was interested _____ office management.

10. I need 40 credits _____ the Humanities.

10 GAMES

1. Careers. *Divide the class into teams of 3–5 students. Have the teams take turns giving clues from the Interest Inventory (paragraph 7), and guessing the career that fits the clues.*

Example:

Team 1 (books open). The person I'm thinking of is observant, logical, analytical, inquisitive, and accurate. What career should this person follow?

Team 2 (books closed). *Begin by asking for clues.*

Does this person like reasoning and making logical decisions?

Does this person like to investigate scientific principles?

Then this person should follow a scientific career.

[*Rules:* The opposing team is allowed three guesses. If it fails to guess correctly, the play continues with the next team.

Scoring: A point is given for each correct guess. The team with the most points wins.]

Continue the practice until all teams have participated.

2. More Careers. *Use the list of careers in paragraph 11. Before the game begins, have each team select a specific career from the list and prepare a list of personality traits, perhaps including some new but appropriate traits in addition to those already studied.*

When play begins, the opposing team must ask for clues. The game proceeds as before.

3. Different Careers. *Before the game begins, each team selects a career that has not been mentioned so far, and prepares a list of personality traits. The opposing team asks for clues. If it fails to guess the career in three attempts, it forfeits, and play moves to the next team.*

11 SKITS *The Job Interview*

1. *Divide the class into small groups. Have each group imagine a job opening, set up an interview, and choose an interviewer and job applicant. Have the interviewer describe the job opening in detail, asking the applicant if he or she has the required job skills,* *education, and experience. The applicant answers the questions, describing his or her educational background and work experience. The applicant might then take a turn asking questions about salary, fringe benefits, promotion policy, whether the company offers equal opportunity to men and women, and the like. After practicing in groups, have the students present their skits before the class.*

2. *As a variation, have the interviewer pretend to be suspicious, ill-humored, hard to please. The applicant must use all his skill and diplomacy to overcome every obstacle and get the job.*

12 CONTROLLED COMPOSITION *Rewrite the selection below. Two ways are provided. Follow the directions in each step.*

Finding a Job

¹Jack believed that intelligent men from his country should be engineers. ²Jack himself had this goal, too. ³He read every book on engineering he could get his hands on. ⁴He talked to his friends, his teachers, and his neighbors. ⁵They told him to major in engineering at school. ⁶They advised him to get a summer job that would give him some engineering experience.

⁷Jack took their advice. ⁸He wrote to the Ajax Company himself, asking for a part-time job. ⁹He received an answer almost immediately. ¹⁰It said, we need a male engineer who is good in math and statistics. ¹¹Jack replied happily, "I'm your man."

1. Rewrite the selection, changing "Jack" to "Betty." Make all other necessary changes. Your first sentence will say:

> Betty believed that intelligent women from her country should be engineers.

2. Rewrite the selection in the negative. Reverse the sense of each sentence to give it the opposite meaning by changing the *principal verbs* from the affirmative to the negative. Your first sentence will say:

> Jack did not believe that intelligent men from his country should be engineers.

13 *FREE COMPOSITION: LETTER WRITING*

A. Formal Letters

1. Pretend there is a job opening in your field. Write a letter applying for this position. Study the model in paragraph 14. Make up an imaginary address. Tell where you learned about the job, and give your qualifications. Conclude by asking for an interview. Be careful of punctuation. Neatness is crucial in letter writing.

2. Write a letter asking for information about a career that interests you. Address it to the U.S. Department of Labor, Washington, D.C., or to an agency in your country. Explain why you like this career, and tell what additional information or other help you need.

B. Informal Letter

3. Write to a friend in your country, describing your new job. Tell how you heard about the job, describe your interview, and tell about your work. Add any other details of interest.

14 *DICTATION*

1. Choosing a career isn't easy.
2. Explore your choice of occupation from every angle.
3. Collect as much information as you can.
4. If you can't stand the sight of blood, don't be a doctor.
5. Be a scientist if you like science and math.
6. Typing and filing are useful business skills.
7. Discuss your program with a school counselor.
8. Get some on-the-job experience.
9. Engineering is nontraditional for women.
10. People who know themselves find the best jobs.

Nine

TAKING STOCK OF YOUR FAMILY FINANCES

Americans, supposedly, live in an affluent society. A comfortable, middle-class existence has become so common, it is taken for granted. A home in the suburbs, the children in college, a car in the garage—these seem to be everyone's idea of success, the American dream come true. But some families never seem to succeed. Although the husband has a good job, the family income disappears without anyone's knowing how or where. Soon the family goes into debt. Their dream has gone up in smoke. The Robinsons in the story that follows are a family like this. Can you find the mistakes they make in money management?

(1) MR. ROBINSON: "I have an idea! Let's buy a station wagon and take the kids to California!"

MRS. ROBINSON: "That's a fine idea, but it's only an idea! How can we afford it?"

MR. ROBINSON: "Oh, we can manage somehow. We can always take out a loan. And of course we also have our credit cards."

(2) And so it goes. Many American families live beyond their means. It's so easy to take out a loan at the bank. Almost any property of value will serve as collateral. And loans up to $1500 can often be made on the strength of a signature alone. Then there is the credit card. That is the little plastic identification plate that you carry in your wallet. Credit cards are issued by banks, travel

He's maxed out

agencies, and credit associations of all kinds. When paying for a meal in a restaurant or buying something in a store, you merely produce your card and say, "Charge it!" Of course you have to pay the bills eventually, but the availability of so much easy credit does make it simple to get over your head in debt.

(3)   Our capitalistic society is based on mass consumption of goods and services of all kinds, and there are so many attractive things to buy. Take the Robinson family, for example. They borrowed several thousand dollars from a bank, bought the camper, assembled a complete set of camping equipment, put a collapsible boat on the roof of their car, and away they went in the general direction of California. Fine. But when the trip was over and the bills started coming in, that was a different story. Payments became due on the car, and the credit card company demanded *immediate* payment of bills for merchandise, gifts, even gasoline and service on their car during the two-week vacation out West. Unfortunately, Mr. Robinson did not have the ready cash to meet these obligations.

(4)   What did the Robinsons do wrong? Was the family income too low? Or did they mismanage what money they had? From the story, you can see how dangerous it is to misuse credit. A little financial planning—keeping an account

The Robinsons bought a station wagon and a camper—on credit.

This couple is making up the weekly budget. What will happen if their income doesn't cover their expenditures?

of income and outgo—will help most families avoid the headaches, and the heartaches too, of even temporary insolvency. There is no one best way of money management for all families, but many could avoid financial problems by the simple expedient of keeping a budget.

(5)   A budget is a working plan for allocating the family finances during the year. It will give you a picture of the family's financial status during a given period of time.

(6)   The first step in budgeting is to estimate your income for the coming year (you may start that "year" at any point) and note when the money will be coming in. Take into account such items as salaries, interest on a bank account, dividends from stocks and bonds, pensions, repayment of a debt to you, and income from "moonlighting"; that is, from a personal business or extra job you may have on the side.

(7)   These monies come in at different times. Salaries, for instance, may be received weekly, biweekly, or monthly; while interest, dividends, and the like are generally credited quarterly. Keeping all this in mind, lay out a schedule of receipts on a periodic basis, either weekly, semimonthly, or monthly.

(8)   The next step, not as pleasant as the first but just as important, is to estimate your expenditures—money you will spend for necessities, for emergencies, or set aside for entertainment. These expenditures fit into two categories— fixed expenses, which occur at predictable intervals; and flexible or optional expenses, which vary from month to month.

(9)   Among the fixed expenditures are such budgetary items as rent, food

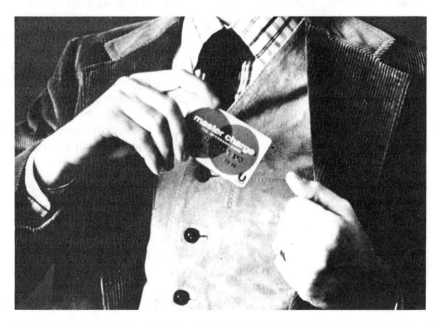

Top: This computer shows your bank balance. Bottom: A credit card is a little plastic identification plate.

bills, the mortgage, and the various premiums for insurance on your health, life, home, and automobile. Fixed expenditures also include such things as tuition payments for education, and installment payments like the ones the Robinsons had on their camper. Other living expenses should be itemized also: laundry, dry cleaning, transportation, newspapers and magazines, education, and, perhaps, household help.

(*10*)   The flexible expenditures involve such items as clothing, new furniture, a new car, and so forth—in other words, items whose expense is entirely up to you and may result from a whim, a sudden urge, or an unexpected need. It is also a good idea to set aside an amount for medical expenses that would not be covered by whatever medical insurance you may have. What if you or a member of your family became ill suddenly? A budgetary allowance should be made for such contingencies. And don't forget to include a certain amount for entertainment.

(*11*)   Once you have planned your budget, it would be a good idea to make up a family balance sheet. A balance sheet is a list of your assets and liabilities. It provides an excellent picture of your current financial status.

(*12*)   Assets include cash on hand as well as what you have in the bank. The value of your car and home should be listed. So should the worth of your furniture, appliances, clothes, jewelry, sports equipment, cameras, and any other items of value. The amount someone owes you is an asset.

(*13*)   Liabilities are what you owe—the unpaid portion of the mortgage on your house, the car loan, charge-account balances, income-tax payments, and any cash borrowing you have done.

(*14*)   The difference between your assets and liabilities is your net worth.

(*15*)   From year to year, your net worth will probably grow, but it may not increase fast enough to suit you. Keeping a budget generally helps people become more conscious of their spending habits. The figures on your ledger will flash a warning signal when your outlays begin to dangerously exceed your income. Many families, as the Robinsons learned, find this an excellent way to grow in net worth from year to year.

Exercises

(*1*) **SCANNING**   *To do this exercise, glance at the text for information, then, eyes up, give the response.*

1. Letting one student be Mr. Robinson and the other Mrs. Robinson, repeat as closely as possible the dialogue at the beginning of the reading.
2. How do many families live?

3. What is so easy to take out?
4. What can serve as collateral?
5. What can be made on the strength of a signature alone?
6. What is a credit card?
7. Which institutions issue credit cards?
8. What do you say when using a credit card?
9. When do you have to pay the bills?
10. What is our capitalistic society based on?
11. How much money did the Robinson family borrow?
12. What did they buy with the money?
13. What kind of boat did they put on the roof of their car?
14. What happened when the bills started coming in?
15. What did the Robinsons do wrong?
16. How can most families avoid temporary insolvency?
17. What is a budget?
18. What is the first step in budgeting?
19. What items should you take into account?
20. Which monies come in at different times?
21. When are salaries received?
22. What is the next step in budgeting?
23. What are expenditures?
24. Which are the fixed expenditures?
25. Which are the flexible expenditures?

2 **VOCABULARY DEVELOPMENT**   *Study the following words. The paragraph from which each word comes is numbered. After studying these words, do exercise 3.*

taking stock (*title*)	**collateral** (*2*)	**insolvency** (*4*)
live beyond your means (*2*)	**on the strength of** (*2*)	**expedient** (*4*)
	to get in over your head (*2*)	**"moonlighting"** (*6*)
take out (*2*)		**contingencies** (*10*)

1. **To take stock of** your finances means to make an inventory of your total worth. You find out what your financial condition is—how much money you have and how much you owe.
2. **To live beyond your means** is to spend more money than you earn, to go into debt in order to buy luxuries you can't afford.

3. **To take out** a loan is to borrow money.
4. **Collateral** is anything of value, like jewelry or cameras, that can be held by the lender to guarantee repayment of a loan.
5. When a person borrows **on the strength of** his or her signature alone, no collateral is needed. One's credit is good. The lender is confident that the loan will be repaid on time.
6. When you **get in over your head,** you undertake a project that is beyond your means. The Robinsons got in over their heads when they bought more than they could afford.
7. **Insolvency** is the condition of being unable to pay off debts, bankrupt.
8. An **expedient** is a practical way of doing something. "Many people avoid financial problems by the simple **expedient** of keeping a budget."
9. **"Moonlighting"** means having a second job for extra income. This work is often done at night, "under the light of the moon"; hence the term "moonlighting."
10. **Contingencies** are possible but unexpected expenses, liable but not certain to occur. Thus the Robinsons decided to put aside money for medical expenses "and other contingencies."

③ *VOCABULARY PRACTICE   Fill in the blank spaces, using the vocabulary words above. Choose words with meanings suggested by the italicized words in parentheses.*

Before going to the bank for a loan, Jack (*made an inventory*) took stock of

his finances. He discovered that he had been (*spending more than he earned*)

and that he had no (*jewelry or other valuables*) collateral to give the

bank. During the year, he had borrowed small amounts from his friends and

(*had spent a lot more than he earned*) gotten in over his head. He was (*bankrupt*) Insolvency.

Fortunately, his reputation was good, so the bank loaned him more money (*on

the basis of*) on the strenght of his signature alone. Jack promised to (*get a second job*)

Moonlight to earn extra money with which to pay back the loan.

4 VOCABULARY   *From the list below, select the word that best completes each sentence and write it in the blank space. Do not use any word more than once.*

mortgage   creditor   net worth
quarterly   available   debtor
capitalistic   budget   ledger
annuity   wallet   credit card

1. I always carry my money in my ___wallet___.

2. If someone owes you money, you are a ___creditor___.

3. If you owe someone money, you are a ___debtor___.

4. At a bank, interest is paid every three months. That means the interest is paid on a ___quarterly___ basis.

5. The book in which you record your finances is called a ___ledger___.

6. A country that believes in the private ownership of banks and factories has a ___capitalistic___ system.

7. When credit is easy to get, it is readily ___available___.

8. What identification do you carry in your wallet when you want to charge purchases at a store? A ___credit card___

9. An ___annuity___ is an amount of money paid to you on a regular basis, often by an insurance company.

10. A plan for spending the family income is called a ___budget___.

5 **VOCABULARY PRACTICE**   *Circle the letter (a, b, or c) in front of the answer that has the same meaning as the italicized word in the sentence.*

1. How much money do you want to *borrow?*
   a. lend
   b. take now and repay later
   c. give away

2. Don't let your wants *exceed* your resources.
   a. be greater than
   b. be equal to
   c. be less than

3. I thought the idea was quite *feasible.*   [fisebol]
   a. weak
   b. possible
   c. impossible

4. Make an *estimate* of the cost first.   [estimate]
   a. approximation
   b. repayment
   c. category

5. He paid for the car in *installments.*
   a. at regular times
   b. in one payment
   c. never paid

6. Try to increase your *assets.*   [asets]
   a. liabilities
   b. cash and property
   c. taxes

7. Some expenditures are the result of a *whim.*   [huim]
   gastos
   a. need
   b. sudden fancy
   c. debt

8. Keep a little money on hand for *contingencies.*
   a. fixed payments
   b. plans
   c. unexpected events

ignorar *Limite de pago*

9. Don't *neglect* to mark the date when loans are due. [du]
   a. hesitate
   b. hasten
   c. fail

10. Some families find themselves in temporary *insolvency*.
    a. with too much money
    b. with no money
    c. with unexpected money

11. With a budget, you can avoid a lot of *anguish*. [anguish] *dolor*
    a. agony
    b. extra payments
    c. imbalance

12. He did not have enough money to pay his *tuition*. [tuishon]
    a. mortgage
    b. school fees
    c. collateral

6 WORD-FORM CHART *Study the following words.*

PARTICIPLE	NOUN	VERB	ADJECTIVE	ADVERB
credited crediting	credit creditor	credit		
	affluence		affluent	
	availability		available	
consumed consuming	consumption consumer	consume		
exceeded exceeding	excess	exceed	excessive	excessively
financed financing	finance	finance	financial	financially
necessitated necessitating	necessity	necessitate	necessary	necessarily

PARTICIPLE	NOUN	VERB	ADJECTIVE	ADVERB
flexed flexing	flexibility	flex	flexible	flexibly
	entirety		entire	entirely
	eventuality		eventual	eventually
described describing	description	describe	descriptive	descriptively
neglected neglecting	neglect	neglect	neglectful	neglectfully
budgeted budgeting	budget	budget	budgetary	
obliged obliging	obligation	oblige	obligatory	
managed managing	management manager	manage	management	
allocated allocating	allocation	allocate		
estimated estimating	estimation estimate	estimate		
	period		periodic	periodically
installed installing	installment installation	install		
paid paying	payment pay	pay	payable	
itemized itemizing	item	itemize		
allowed allowing	allowance	allow	allowable	
	capital capitalism capitalist		capitalistic capital	

7 **WORD-FORM PRACTICE**   *In the blank space, write the correct form of the italicized word.*

1. *entirety*   I think the ___entire___ book is dull.

2. *excessive*   His work will ___exceed___ our expectations.

3. *flexibility*   He showed ___flexibility___ in a very difficult situation.

4. *capital*   Most Western economies are based on the ___capitalist___ system.

5. *necessary*   Food is a ___necessity___.

6. *budgetary*   Keeping a ___budget___ makes good sense.

7. *pay*   I expect full ___payment___ for my work.

8. *oblige*   He fulfilled all his ___obligations___.

9. *estimated*   Give me an ___estimate___ of the cost of these auto repairs.

10. *finance*   Having lost all his money, Bill was in ___financial___ difficulty.

11. *exceed*   These costs are ___excessive___.

12. *manage*   The ___manager___ at the bank gave him a mortgage.

13. *pay*   The final ___payment___ on the mortgage is due this month.

14. *allow*   Each child in the family receives an ___allowance___ every week.

15. *item*   ___itemize___ these figures, please.

16. *oblige*   Is this punctuation optional or ___obligatory___?

17. *management*   Did she ___manage___ to find a new job?

18. *describe*   Give me a ___description___ of the girl sitting next to you.

19. *flex* Are the terms of this loan ~~flexible~~ or in~~flexible~~ (one word)?

20. *oblige* Frances can easily meet all her ~~obligation~~ this year.

21. *eventual* ~~eventually~~ we'll get married.

22. *finance* His ~~financial~~ condition is good.

23. *describe* The novel was highly ~~descriptive~~ *adj*

24. *affluence* We live in an ~~affluent~~ society. [sosaiety] *adj*

25. *period* Exams will be given in this course ~~periodically~~ *adv.*

[piriodicli]

8 **PARTICIPLES** *In the blank space, write the correct form of the participle.*

1. *credit* The correctly _____ amount was deposited in the bank.

2. *oblige* The _____ waitress helped the girl with her coat.

3. *itemize* _____ figures won't be ready until Monday.

4. *neglect* The _____ child had been abandoned by its parents.

5. *allow* Haircuts are an _____ expense in the budget.

6. *finance* His under_____ (one word) business went bankrupt.

7. *manage* A well-_____ pet is delightful.

8. *estimate* Get the _____ figures to me by Wednesday.

9. *consume* The un_____ (one word) part of the house was still standing after the fire.

10. *pay* The under_____ (one word) workers liked their new union contract.

9
PRACTICE WITH PREFIXES Bi-*is a Latin prefix referring to things that come in pairs or happen twice in a given period. In the blank space, explain the meaning of each of the words in the column at the left.*

Example: biannual   an event that comes twice a year
         bicycle   a vehicle with two wheels

1. *bimonthly*   _____

2. *binocular*   _____

3. *biped*   _____

4. *bifocals*   _____

5. *bicentenary*   _____

Semi- *is a prefix meaning half, partially, or not fully. Explain the meaning of each of the words in the column at the left.*

6. *semiconscious*   _____

7. *semiautomatic*   _____

8. *semiskilled*   _____

Un- *is a prefix that makes words negative or gives them the opposite meaning. Using synonyms, explain each of the words below.*

9. *unavoidable*   _____

10. *unconscious*   _____

11. *unclean*   _____

12. *unknown*   _____

13. *unconvinced*   _____

14. *uncoordinated*   _____

15. *uncontrolled*   _____

10
READING COMPREHENSION   *On the basis of the story, mark each of the following sentences T if it is true or F if it is false.*

1. __F__ The Robinsons were good money managers.

2. __T__ The plastic identification plate that you carry in your wallet is called a credit card.

3. __F__ When you charge things at a store, you do *not* have to pay for them eventually.

4. __F__ The Robinsons borrowed money and bought a new house.

5. __T__ Insolvency is a pleasant experience.

6. __T__ A budget is a plan for spending the family income during the year.

7. __F__ The first step in making a budget is to spend as much money as you can.

8. __F__ In setting up a budget, you should only put down your salary, and nothing else.

9. __F__ To moonlight is to take a trip at night—under the moon.

10. __T__ Expenditures are of two kinds—fixed and flexible.

11. __T__ Examples of fixed expenses are the rent, food, and insurance.

12. __T__ Doctors' bills are an unexpected expense.

13. __F__ When a boy and a girl go on a date, that is a fixed expense.

14. __T__ A balance sheet is a list of assets and liabilities.

15. __T__ Assets include such things as a car, home, and jewelry.

11 ***BUDGET PRACTICE*** *A. Look back through the story for all the "fixed" expenditures and for those that are "flexible" and add them to the list below.*

FIXED EXPENSES	FLEXIBLE EXPENSES
1. rent	1. clothing
2. food bills	2. new furniture
3.	3.
4.	4.
5.	5.
6.	6.
7.	7.
8.	8.
9.	9.
10.	10.
11.	11.
12.	12.
13.	13.
14.	14.
15.	15.

B. Correctly classify the following items and add them to the list in section A. Remember that fixed expenses are unavoidable and occur at regular intervals, while flexible expenses are optional.

1. one dollar paid to your neighbor's son for cutting the grass
2. baby-sitting expenses
3. repairs to the television set
4. whiskey for Uncle Joe, who is an alcoholic
5. the electric bill
6. haircuts
7. a new fur coat for the wife
8. a vacation in Puerto Rico
9. payment to the plumber to repair the toilet
10. extras for the new family car, such as power steering and power brakes
11. rent on a house in the country, which the couple needs for relaxing from the tensions of their jobs

C. Now add five items of your own to the list.

12 *ORAL PRACTICE*

THE ROBINSON FAMILY'S MONTHLY BUDGET

Income		Outgo	
Salary: Mr. Robinson	$ 800	*Fixed*	
Mrs. Robinson	550	Rent	$ 555
Interest from bank account	60	Food: vegetables	56
Repayment of loan by Mrs.		meat	72
Robinson's sister	150	Life insurance and other	
Mr. Robinson moonlights in		premiums	60
the evening to earn extra		Tuition payments	85
money	80	Installment charges on car	55
	$1,640	Laundry	14
		Telephone	23
		Flexible	
		Contingency fund	50
		Clothing	40
		Entertainment	40
			$1,050

Questions with "how much?"

1. How much is Mr. Robinson's salary?
2. How much is the food bill? How much would the Robinsons save if they became vegetarians? Ask other questions using "how much?"
3. *Discussion:* Mr. Robinson smokes $35 worth of pipe tobacco each month. "It's my only luxury," he says. Would you classify this as a fixed or flexible expense?

   Mrs. Robinson and the children are food faddists and subscribe to magazines that tell them how to "keep fit," in the amount of $18 per month. How would you classify this expense?

   Discuss other monthly expenses and how they should be classified.

13 *CONTROLLED COMPOSITION* *Rewrite the selection below. Two ways are provided. Follow the directions in each step.*

Mexico

[1]Everyone likes to travel. [2]Last year, the Browns made the trip of a lifetime. [3]They went to Mexico. [4]To afford this trip, they saved for a year. [5]First, they made up a *money plan*. [6]The *plan* showed their income and expenditures. [7]To help out, Mr. Brown *got a second job* at night. [8]The children helped, too. [9]They earned money for *school fees*. [10]The family set aside a small amount for *unexpected events*. [11]They did not misuse their *plastic cards* at the store. [12]Finally, they listed their *cash on hand* and their *debts*. [13]Everything balanced. [14]What a wonderful trip they had seeing Mexico City, Puebla, and Cuernavaca.

1. Pretend that you are going to take this trip next summer. Rewrite the entire selection. Starting with sentence 2, change the verbs from the past tense to the future tense, using *will/shall* or *am going to*. Use *next year* in place of *last year*.
2. Rewrite the selection. Replace the italicized words with synonyms from the lesson.

14 *TOPICS FOR WRITING AND DISCUSSION*

1. Imagine that you are going to take a trip. You have unlimited funds. Describe where you would go and how much money you would allocate for transportation, clothes, restaurants, nightclubs, parties, souvenirs, and so on.
2. Discuss the advantages and disadvantages of keeping a budget.
3. Assume you are giving advice to a friend who has just arrived in this city. He has had no experience in handling money before. He needs to know how much to allocate for food, rent, transportation, entertainment, clothing, and incidentals. He should also keep a cash reserve in the bank. How would you advise him?
4. Does the capitalistic society encourage people to be extravagant? What changes in our economic system would you recommend?
5. For some people, spending money is a bad habit. They cannot save, so they are always broke. Tell how you would help such a person.
6. Explain your own system for money management.

15 DICTATION

1. Bert borrowed money on the strength of his signature.
2. A capitalistic society is based on mass consumption.
3. His camping equipment included a collapsible boat.
4. After the trip, the bills came in.
5. They bought too much merchandise.
6. Allocate some money for entertainment.
7. Make an estimate of your budget.
8. Do you receive any pensions and annuities?
9. Some salaries are biweekly.
10. A mortgage is a fixed expense.

Ten

SKI TOURING

A Fast-Growing Sport

People in tropical countries can read about winter sports but are unable to participate in them. They cannot build snowmen, throw snowballs, toboggan, or ice skate. Above all, they cannot go skiing.

Someone defined skiing as gliding over the ground on two boards. The sport is popular in the U.S. in the states that have snow in the winter months. The pleasure we take in this healthy outdoor activity is shared by the Finns, the Russians, the Swedes, the Norwegians, the Germans, the Italians, the Swiss, and the French, who also live in temperate zones with winter climates. But what must people from Egypt, Libya, and Nigeria think of this strange sport?

Skiing, unlike tennis and baseball, is not a city sport. Until recently, even in countries with snow, it was limited to mountainous regions. Now there is a new variation that can be enjoyed by everyone. It is called ski touring.

(1)   More than 4,000 years ago, a primitive artist carved a crude portrait on the side of a rock in northern Norway. The carving portrayed a man on a pair of skis. Today, more than a million Americans have something in common with that Stone Age character—they have joined in a fast-growing sport called "ski touring."

(2)   My wife, Tina, and I have been "touring" for four years now. This makes us veterans in a sport that has become popular only recently, but is already among the fastest-growing sports in America. Ski touring is easy,

healthy, cheap, unpretentious fun—and an ideal winter family activity. There are several things it is not.

(3)   Touring definitely isn't racing at top speed over the countryside on skis. That is called cross-country skiing, which is a more demanding sport and requires first-class physical condition and a good deal of stamina. Ski touring is not the Alpine or downhill variety either. That branch of the sport requires a mountain. It is practiced in mountainous regions like the central massif in Norway, the Alps in Switzerland, and the slopes of the Appalachians or the Rockies in the United States.

(4)   To a ski tourer, the joy of this sport lies in its simplicity. It can be enjoyed wherever there is snow on an open field or road. When the snow falls, the tourer grabs a pair of wooden skis, puts on hiking boots and old clothes, and heads for the nearest suitable spot. This could be the local golf course, for instance, closed to golfers in the winter and covered with snow drifts. There are no long rides over icy roads; no interminable waits in ski-lift lines; no fancy stretch pants, $100 ski boots, or $200 skis.

(5)   Ski touring is really a lot like hiking, except that if you do it right, it isn't as tiring. The equipment is practical, durable, and light. There are no fashion shows on the ski-touring trail.

(6)   Skis can cost anywhere from $15 to $60, depending upon size and quality. There are special ski-touring boots, but ordinary hiking boots or work shoes can be used just as well.

(7)   Clothing is casual and uncomplicated. Ski tourers generate plenty of body heat once under way and are seldom bothered by cold. Trousers should be loose and comfortable. Many ski tourers wear knickers or knee pants, which have become a symbol of the sport. But any tightly woven, loose-fitting pair of pants will do as well.

(8)   "If you can walk, you can ski tour," is one of the sport's clichés. This is a bit of oversimplification, for there is a technique to ski touring, a kick-and-glide motion that enables you to cover a lot of ground with a little effort.

(9)   To get an idea of basic ski-touring technique, try to imagine that instead of skis you're wearing old-fashioned bedroom slippers and are shuffling along on a newly waxed floor. Your heels may turn a bit, but as long as your toes are touching the front of the slipper, things are under control.

(10)   This is not only a good image, but it's also a good ski-touring exercise. If you can take long strides across a slippery floor, you can master ski touring.

(11)   Touring skis fasten at the boot tip, leaving the heels free. To someone used to downhill skis, this makes them feel half on. When parallel with each other, they feel and are very unstable.

(12)   The stablest position is with one ski thrust well in front of the other. So, the ski tourer strides along, alternatively sliding one ski and then the other in front of him. To pick up speed, he thrusts with his poles and uses a kicking technique similar to that used by ice skaters.

Ski tourers wear casual clothes—a jacket or parka, pants, and boots.

(13) Lifting up a heel, he thrusts one ski back while pushing the other forward. The back of the kicking ski is raised in the air with the front tip touching the snow. By rapidly alternating skis, he produces a graceful ground-eating glide that from a distance looks as if he's running across the snow.

(14) On one of our first ski-touring trips together, we joined a group for a day in New Hampshire. Tina, with some previous touring experience, was able to keep up with the main party. I, using borrowed equipment and with very little time on touring skis, walked, stumbled, and staggered at the rear, getting progressively farther and farther behind.

(15) Fortunately, as the sun was setting and the temperature plummeting, Tina raced ahead and stopped a passing snowmobile club, which came roaring out of the woods and rescued me and several other very tired novice tourers.

Being rescued is humiliating, particularly when the rescuers are devotees of a rival sport. But freezing to death isn't much fun either.

(*16*)   We learned a lesson and now take care not to exceed our strength or ability, both of which have improved a lot since that nightmarish incident. As in almost any other outdoor activity, common sense is an important part of one's basic equipment.

(*17*)   That ski touring is easy to master is obvious from the sport's phenomenal growth. In the three years from 1977 to 1979, only about 50,000 touring skis were sold in the U.S., whereas in 1985 alone Americans bought more than 350,000 pairs of these skis, most of them imported from Scandinavia.

(*18*)   As ski touring grows more popular, facilities for the sport are expanding, too. There are now chains of commercial ski-touring centers—each usually with its own network of marked trails—renting and selling equipment and providing instruction. While some members of the family may be chicken* about schussing† down mountainsides, today everybody can go on a touring trip.

Exercises

1
SCANNING   *To do this exercise, glance at the text for information, then, eyes up, give the response.*

  1. How long ago was the crude portrait carved?
  2. What kind of artist carved the portrait?
  3. On what was the portrait carved?
  4. In which country was the portrait carved?
  5. What did the carving portray?
  6. How many Americans share something with that primitive man?
  7. What is it that they share with him?
  8. Who does the author go touring with?
  9. How many years has the author been touring?
 10. What does this make him?
 11. Describe ski touring.
 12. When defining ski touring, the author says that it is not several things. What are they?
 13. Where is Alpine skiing practiced?

*American slang, meaning timid or cowardly.
†A ski term from the German, meaning a straight, high-speed run.

14. Where does the joy of ski touring lie?
15. Where can it be enjoyed?
16. What does the tourer grab when the snow falls?
17. What does the tourer put on?
18. What does the tourer head for?
19. What does the ski tourer avoid?
20. What is the tourer's equipment like?
21. How much do skis cost?
22. What does the price depend on?
23. What kind of boots does the tourer wear?
24. What is casual and uncomplicated?
25. What do ski tourers generate?
26. When do they generate it?
27. What trousers are best for this sport?
28. What is a symbol of this sport?
29. What motion or technique do tourers use?
30. Using this motion, how much ground can they cover?
31. To practice this technique, what can you wear instead of skis?
32. What kind of slippers are you wearing?
33. What movement are you making on the waxed floor?
34. What may turn a bit during this movement?
35. For things to be under control, what must be touching the front of the slipper?
36. What kind of strides must you take across the floor?
37. Where do touring skis fasten?
38. What is left free?
39. How does this make the boots feel?
40. What are placed parallel to each other?

2 **VOCABULARY DEVELOPMENT** *Study the following words. The paragraph from which each word comes is numbered. After studying these words, do exercise 3.*

unpretentious (*2*)	**shuffle** (*9*)	**stagger** (*14*)
stamina (*3*)	**stride** (*10*)	**phenomenal** (*17*)
generate (*7*)	**fasten** (*11*)	
under way (*7*)	**glide** (*13*)	

1. An **unpretentious** person is simple, humble.

2. When a person has **stamina,** he or she has energy, great endurance, and staying power. "Karen revealed unexpected **stamina** by hiking twenty miles."

3. To **generate** is to create or produce something. "A generator **generates** electricity."

4. When someone gets **under way,** that person gets into motion, starts doing something or going somewhere. "If we are going to the movies tonight, let's get **under way.**"

5. To **shuffle** is to walk slowly, dragging the feet. "Jack, who was old and tired, walked with a **shuffle.**"

6. To **stride** is to walk with long steps.

7. To **fasten** is to attach. "**Fasten** the door so that it won't blow open."

8. To **glide** is to move gently and smoothly, with an unbroken motion. "Birds **glide** through the air; fish **glide** through the sea."

9. To **stagger** is to walk unevenly, to sway, to have trouble standing upright. "Vicky could hardly walk because she was **staggering** so badly."

10. **Phenomenal** means extraordinary, unusual. "Pete had **phenomenal** success in his first year at school."

3 **VOCABULARY PRACTICE**   *Fill in the blank spaces, using the vocabulary words above.*

1. How much electricity does this battery _____?

2. After drinking ten glasses of whiskey, Betty _____ out of the room and down the street.

3. Here is a hammer and nails. _____ these boards together.

4. The British Grenadiers take very long _____ when they march before Buckingham Palace.

5. Steve was able to swim for hours. His _____ was amazing.

6. A snake _____ over the ground silently and without effort.

7. Betty, who was modest, shy, and unassuming, was considered very

   _____ by her friends.

8. The economic recovery of West Germany after World War II was simply

   _____.

9. It's time to go, so let's get _____.

10. Walter was so tired he dragged his feet all the way home. He walked with a

    _____.

4
VOCABULARY   *Circle the answer (a, b, or c) most similar in meaning to the italicized word.*

1. The artist carved a *crude* portrait.
   a. rough and unfinished
   b. modern
   c. historical

2. We are *veterans* of this sport.
   a. experienced people
   b. wealthy people
   c. city people

3. The wait for the bus was *interminable*.
   a. endless
   b. short
   c. pleasant

4. His statement was an *oversimplification* of the facts.
   a. too simple
   b. too complicated
   c. not understandable

5. There is a definite *technique* to ski touring.
   a. clothing
   b. equipment
   c. method

6. Are your skis *parallel* to each other?
   a. above
   b. side by side
   c. below

7. He was wearing bedroom *slippers*.
   a. pajamas
   b. shoes
   c. robes

8. The best technique is to *thrust* one ski ahead of the other.
   a. push
   b. pull
   c. throw

9. When skiing, lift up the *heel*.
   a. back of the foot
   b. side of the foot
   c. front of the foot

10. My pace was slow, and I got *progressively* farther behind.
   a. gradually by degrees
   b. rapidly
   c. noticeably

11. Ski touring is easy *to master*.
   a. to slide
   b. to learn
   c. to glide

12. Do not *exceed* your strength on a ski hike.
   a. go beyond the limits of
   b. increase
   c. decrease

13. The author felt *humiliated* to be rescued by a snowmobile.
   a. embarrassed
   b. cold
   c. happy

14. *Facilities* for ski touring are expanding.
   a. mountainsides
   b. special locations and equipment
   c. carvings

15. Facilities for this sport are *expanding*.
   a. getting larger
   b. getting smaller
   c. staying the same

5
SYNONYMS   *Rewrite the following sentences, replacing the word or phrase in italics with the best synonym from the list. Do not use any synonym more than once.*

under way	fancy	nightmare
stamina	humiliating	novices
interminable	parallel	fasten
plummeted	durable	stretch pants
drifts	portrait	phenomenal

1. These hiking shoes are *long-lasting.*
2. Let's get *started.*
3. *Attach* those two boards together.
4. Each winter, snow accumulates in large *piles* on the road.
5. Ed has great *endurance.* He can walk for miles.
6. Sally likes very *ornate* clothing.
7. Last night Carmen had a *bad dream.*
8. Hank and his wife were *beginners* at tennis.
9. The stone *fell* to the ground.
10. Ski touring has enjoyed *amazing* growth in recent years.

6
VERB PRACTICE   *From the list below, select the verb that best completes each sentence and write it in the blank space. Do not use any verb more than once.*

generates	rescued	head for
thrust	glide	strides
grab	staggered	carved
shuffling		

1. When Jack walks, he usually takes long steps. That is, he _____ across the floor.

2. Sometimes Jack drags his feet. Then he is _____ across the floor.

3. When I work hard, my body _____ lots of heat.

4. The artist _____ a statue out of stone.

5. When skiing, you must _____ one foot ahead of the other.

6. Arlene saw Bill struggling in the water. She jumped in and _____ him immediately.

7. Jack had been drinking beer and could hardly walk. He _____ down the street.

8. The art of good skiing is to _____ over the snow.

9. On a hot day in summer, I _____ the nearest swimming pool.

10. When I get to the pool, I _____ my bathing suit and go in for a swim.

7 WORD-FORM CHART *Study the following words.*

PARTICIPLE	NOUN	VERB	ADJECTIVE	ADVERB
carved carving	carving	carve		
portrayed portraying	portrait	portray		
skied skiing	ski skier	ski		
simplified simplifying	simplicity	simplify	simple	simply
hiked hiking	hike hiker	hike		
	mountain		mountainous	
slipped slipping	slip	slip	slippery	
endured enduring	durability	endure	durable	durably
complicated complicating	complication	complicate		
humiliated humiliating	humility humiliation	humiliate	humble	humbly

8 WORD-FORM PRACTICE   *In the blank space, write the correct form of the italicized word.*

1. *carve*   Michael bought a lovely _____ from a sculptor.

2. *hiking*   Let's take a _____.

3. *mountain*   Skiing is done on hilly or _____ terrain.

4. *slip*   Soapy water has a _____ feeling.

5. *durable*   Does love _____ forever?

6. *ski*   Are you a good _____?

7. *portray*   Paint my _____, please.

8. *humiliation*   The teacher _____ Jane by ignoring her.

9. *complicate*   In life it is best to avoid all _____.

10. *slip*   Frank _____ on the freshly waxed floor.

11. *endure*   _____ is a quality desired in manufactured goods.

12. *simple*   Abe Lincoln was known for his _____.

13. *hike*   Who is the best _____ you know?

14. *simple*   Can you _____ this problem?

15. *humiliate*   _____ is a terrible feeling.

9 PREPOSITIONS   *Insert the correct preposition in each blank space.*

1. José found a carving _____ a man _____ a cave.

2. Skiing is the process _____ gliding _____ the snow.

3. José slipped _____ the ice and fell _____ the snow.

4. The skier puts _____ his boots and grabs his skis.

5. Does a ski tourer have to wait _____ line _____ a ski lift?

6. No, she grabs a pair _____ skis and heads _____ the nearest open field.

7. Fasten touring skis _____ the boot tip, not _____ the heel _____ the shoe.

8. When parallel _____ each other, skis feel unstable.

9. The author went _____ his wife _____ many enjoyable outings.

10. Ski touring is gaining _____ popularity _____ the United States.

10

PREFIX EXERCISE *The meaning of words is changed by the addition of a prefix. Complete the list below by finding all the words in the story that change their meaning in this way. Provide a definition for each word, and then use the word in a sentence of your own.*

WORDS WITH PREFIXES	DEFINITION	ORIGINAL SENTENCE
*un*pretentious		
*in*terminable		
*un*complicated		

11

READING COMPREHENSION *On the basis of the story, mark each of the following sentences T if it is true or F if it is false.*

1. ____ Ski touring is the fastest-growing sport in the U.S.

2. ____ This sport is a form of downhill or Alpine skiing.

3. ____ A ski tourer may enjoy this sport wherever there is snow on an open field.

4. ____ Ski-touring fashions include fancy stretch pants.

5. ____ The rest of the equipment is expensive and complicated.

6. ____ Since touring is a winter sport, skiers are bothered by the cold.

7. ____ A kick-and-glide motion is a good technique for covering a lot of ground.

8. ____ If you can wear bedroom slippers, you can ski.

9. ____ The author had to be rescued by a snowmobile because he broke a ski.

10. ____ Ski touring is a dangerous sport and difficult to learn.

12 ***CONTROLLED COMPOSITION***   *Read the selection below. Then follow the directions in each step.*

The Olympics

[1]The Olympic Games began in ancient Greece. [2]Every four years, Greek athletes assembled at Olympia, a city in western Greece. [3]The athletes dedicated themselves to the high ideals of sports, and competed in different events. [4]The winners each received a gold crown of olive leaves. [5]The Olympics lasted over a thousand years, from 776 B.C. to A.D. 393. [6]Then, as civilization declined, they disappeared.

[7]The Games were not revived until modern times. [8]The Greeks staged the first modern Olympics in Athens, in 1896. [9]In 1900, the Games were held in Paris. [10]And, unless interrupted by war, they have been held every four years since. [11]In 1984, the Olympics were staged in Los Angeles.

1. Question practice: Make up questions for each sentence, using question words such as *did, what, when, where, who, how often.* Can you make up three questions (or more) for each sentence? For example:

> The Olympic Games began in ancient Greece.
> A. Did the Olympic Games begin in Greece?
> B. What began in Greece?
> C. Where did the Olympic Games begin?

2. When the questions are finished, have students put them on the blackboard, and then correct each other's work.

13 TOPICS FOR WRITING AND DISCUSSION

1. Tell about an athlete you admire.
2. Describe your favorite sport.
3. In the U.S., women go in for sports that were formerly practiced only by men, joining the men in baseball, tennis, and golf. Some women have experimented with boxing, wrestling, and football. Is this development good for these sports? Do women benefit from participating in these sports? Explain.
4. In the U.S., baseball is the national sport. In many other countries, soccer holds first place. Which is the more interesting game? Explain your opinion.
5. What is the most important game in your country? Explain why it is popular.
6. Describe a sport you have never tried, and tell why it interests you.

14 DICTATION

1. The artist was known for his portraits.
2. Old soldiers are called veterans.
3. We like summer clothing that is casual and uncomplicated.
4. Ski pants are tightly woven and loose fitting.
5. Can you take long strides in slippers?
6. The old man shuffled across the room.
7. Fasten your seat belts, everybody.
8. Swimming is healthy, unpretentious fun.
9. Carl was a cross-country runner.
10. The wait for the bus seemed interminable.

Eleven

POLLUTION IS
A DIRTY WORD

The earth is our home. We must take care of it, for ourselves and for the next generation. This means preserving the quality of our environment.

The importance of this task is stressed by scientists who study the relation of people to nature. These scientists are called *ecologists,* from the Greek word *oikos,* which means home. Ecologists are responsible for keeping the land, air, and water clean. "How are we doing?" an ecologist was asked recently. "Lousy," the scientist said, sniffing the fume-laden air. "We've got to do a better job—and soon—or it will be too late."

(1) Consume, consume, consume! Our society is consumer oriented—dangerously so. To keep the wheels of industry turning, we manufacture consumer goods in endless quantities, and, in the process, are rapidly exhausting our natural resources. But this is only half the problem. What do we do with manufactured products when they are worn out? They must be disposed of, but how and where? Unsightly junkyards full of rusting automobiles already surround every city in the nation. Americans throw away 80 billion bottles and cans each year, enough to build more than 10 stacks to the moon. There isn't room for much more waste, and yet the factories grind on. They cannot stop, because everyone wants a job. Our standard of living, one of the highest in the world, requires the consumption of manufactured products in ever-increasing

amounts. About to be buried in our own waste, we are caught in a vicious cycle. "Stop the world, I want to get off," is the way a popular song put our dilemma.

(2) It wasn't always like this. Only 100 years ago, people lived in harmony with nature. There weren't so many people then, and their wants were fewer. Whatever wastes were produced could be absorbed by nature and were soon covered over. Today this harmonious relationship is threatened by our lack of foresight and planning, and by carelessness and greed. For we are slowly poisoning our environment.

(3) Pollution is a "dirty" word. To pollute means to contaminate—to spoil something by introducing inpurities that make it unfit or unclean to use. Pollution comes in many forms. We *see* it, *smell* it, *taste* it, *drink* it, and *stumble* through it. We literally live in and breathe pollution, and, not surprisingly, it is beginning to threaten our health, our happiness, and our very civilization.

(4) Once we thought of pollution as meaning simply smog*—the choking, stinging, dirty air that hovers over cities. But air pollution, while it is still the most dangerous, is only one type of contamination among several that attack the most basic life functions.

(5) Through the uncontrolled use of insecticides, people have polluted the land, killing the wildlife. By dumping sewage and chemicals into rivers and lakes, we have contaminated our drinking water. We are polluting the oceans, too, killing the fish and thereby depriving ourselves of an invaluable food supply.

(6) Part of the problem is our exploding population. More and more people produce more wastes. But this problem is intensified by our "throwaway" technology. Each year Americans dispose of 7 million autos, 20 million tons of waste paper, 25 million pounds of toothpaste tubes, and 48 million cans. We throw away gum wrappers, newspapers, and paper plates. It is no longer fashionable to reuse anything. Today almost everything is disposable. Instead of repairing a toaster or a radio, it is easier and cheaper to buy a new one and discard the old, even though 95 percent of its parts may still be functioning. Baby diapers, which used to be made of reusable cloth, are now paper throwaways. Soon we will wear clothing made of paper: "Wear it once and throw it away" will be the slogan of the fashion conscious.

(7) Where is this all to end? Are we turning the world into a gigantic dump, or is there hope that we can solve the pollution problem? Fortunately, solutions are in sight. A few of them are positively ingenious.

(8) Take the problem of discarded automobiles, for instance. Each year over 40,000 of them are abandoned in New York City alone. Eventually the discards end up in a junkyard. But cars are too bulky to ship as scrap to a steel mill. They must first be flattened. This is done in a giant compressor that can reduce a Cadillac to the size of a television set in a matter of minutes. Any leftover scrap metal is mixed with concrete and made into exceptionally strong

---

*"Smog" is a composite word formed from the first letters of *smoke* and the last letters of *fog*.

Some cities are surrounded by unsightly junkyards.

Air pollution is a serious problem.

bricks that are used in buildings and bridges. Our ingenuity has come to the rescue.

(9)   What about water pollution? More and more cities are building sewage-treatment plants. Instead of being dumped into a nearby river or lake, sewage is sent through a system of underground pipes to a giant tank where the water is separated from the solid material, purified, and returned for reuse to the community water supply. The solid material, called sludge, is converted into fertilizer. The sludge can also be made into bricks.

(10)   Controlling air pollution is another crucial objective. Without food, we can live about five weeks; without water, about five days. Without air, people can only live five minutes, so pure air is a must. Here the wrongdoer is the automobile. Where there is a concentration of automobiles, as in our big cities, air pollution is severe. It is important to see that our cars are equipped with pollution-control devices. Such devices effectively reduce the harmful gases emitted from the engine.

(11)   Power plants, factories, and apartment buildings can also avoid air pollution. When possible they should use clean fuels such as gas and oil. And the smokestacks of these buildings should be equipped with filters and other smoke-reduction devices.

(12)   Can we eliminate pollution altogether? Probably not. Today we pollute with everything we do, so total elimination would require drastic measures. Every power plant would have to shut down. Industries would have to close. We would have to leave all our automobiles in the garage. Every bus and truck and airplane would have to stop running. There would be no way to bring food to the cities. There would be no heat and no light. Under these conditions, our population would die in a short time.

(13)   Since such a drastic solution is impossible, we must employ determined public action. We can reduce pollution, even if we can't eliminate it altogether. But we must all do our part. Check your car to see if the pollution-control device is working. Reduce your use of electricity. Is air conditioning really necessary? Don't dump garbage or other waste on the land or in the water. Demand that government take firm action against polluters. We can have a clean world or we can do nothing. The choice is up to you.

Exercises

1
SCANNING   *To do this exercise, glance at the text for information, then, eyes up, give the response.*

1. What is consumer oriented? *our society*
2. What do we manufacture? *consumer goods*
3. How many consumer goods do we manufacture? *endless quantities*
4. What <u>harm</u> are we doing in the process? *exhausting our natural resources.*

5. What happens to manufactured goods when they are worn out?
6. What is full of rusting automobiles?
7. What is around every city in the nation?
8. How many bottles do Americans throw away each year?
9. How many stacks will these bottles build?
10. How far will the stacks go?
11. How much room is there for more waste?
12. Why can't the factories stop?
13. What does our standard of living require?
14. Who is about to be buried?
15. What are we caught in?
16. How does the popular song express our dilemma?
17. How long ago did people live in harmony with nature?
18. How many people were there then?
19. What happened to the wastes they produced?
20. What has happened today to this relationship?
21. What are people doing to their environment?
22. What is a dirty word?
23. What does that word mean?
24. How many forms does pollution come in?
25. Tell what these forms are.
26. What is pollution doing to our health?
27. What is smog?
28. What kind of air hovers over our cities?
29. Which type of pollution is the most dangerous?
30. What have we done to the land?
31. Who has killed the wildlife?
32. How have we contaminated our water?
33. Who is polluting the oceans?
34. How are we killing the fish?
35. What is causing part of the problem?

2
VOCABULARY DEVELOPMENT   *Study the following words. The paragraph from which each word comes is numbered. After studying these words, do exercise 3.*

consumer (*1*)	**impurities** (*3*)	**ingenuity** (*7*)
junkyard (*1*)	**stumble** (*3*)	**fertilizer** (*9*)
stack (*1*)	**sewage** (*5*)	**smokestack** (*11*)
dilemma (*1*)		

1. The **consumer** is the person who uses services and manufactured goods.
2. **Sewage** is human waste. In most cities it is sent through a **sewer system** to a **sewage-treatment plant.**
3. A **dilemma** is a problem situation for which there is no desirable solution.
4. A **junkyard** is the place where scrap metal and old cars are discarded.
5. A **stack** is a pile of something, like lumber.
6. **Impurities** are foreign materials that make something unfit for use.
7. To **stumble** is to trip and almost fall.
8. **Smokestacks** are tall chimneys used by factories to discharge smoke into the upper air.
9. **Ingenuity** is cleverness and skill in doing or inventing something.
10. **Fertilizer** is any material that will enrich the soil.

(3) **VOCABULARY PRACTICE**   *Fill in the blank spaces, using the vocabulary words above.*

1. Our car is <u>worn out</u>. It is ready to be thrown in the <u>Junkyard</u>

2. All <u>Impurities</u> must be removed from food before it can be sold.

3. <u>Sewage</u> can be converted into usable material at a <u>Sewage</u> treatment plant.

4. This factory needs taller <u>smokestacks</u>.

5. The student showed great <u>Ingenuity</u> in repairing her car.

6. The man began to run, but he <u>stumbled</u> and nearly fell.

7. Is it true that the <u>Consumer</u> is always cheated by big business?

8. Cow manure is an excellent <u>Fertilizer</u>.

9. How many <u>stacks</u> of pancakes can you eat?

10. We must either restrict our <u>wastes</u> or accept pollution. This is our <u>dilemma</u>.

④ **VOCABULARY**   *From the list below, select the word that best completes each sentence and write it in the blank space. Do not use any word more than once.*

examen

wastes	harmony	bulky
disposable	wrappers	severe
plates	slogan	buried
scrap	smog	radio
sewage	unfit	power plant
foresight	pollution	junkyards
tubes	diapers	

1. Polluted water is __unfit__ for human use.

2. A married couple must live in __harmony__ if both are to be happy.

3. We lack __foresight__ in planning for the future.

4. Human __wastes__ are discharged into the sewage system.

5. The dirty air that accumulates over cities is called __smog__

6. __disposable__ products are manufactured to be used once and then thrown away.

7. To end air __pollution__ we must control auto emissions.

8. Waste material is called __scrap__.

9. Toothpaste comes in __tubes__.

10. Babies customarily use many __diapers__.

11. Gum __wrappers__ are often thrown on the sidewalk.

12. People are about to be __buried__ in their own wastes.

13. Water from the __sewage__ system can be purified and reused, thanks to modern science.

14. Electricity is manufactured in a __power plant__

15. A picnic lunch is usually eaten off paper __plates__.

5 IDIOMS AND SPECIAL EXPRESSIONS *In the blank, insert the word that completes the expression.*

1. To have jobs for everyone, we must keep the wheels of industry _turning_.

2. Manufactured products that are worn out must be disposed _of_.

3. We are caught in a _vicious_ cycle.

4. We live in a "throw-_away_" society.

5. There isn't room for much more waste, yet the factories grind _on_.

6. Our society is consumer _oriented_.

7. Our _standard_ of living is the highest in the world.

8. Discarded automobiles end _up_ in the junkyard.

9. Left _over_ (one word) scrap metal can be made into bricks.

10. To eliminate pollution, every power plant would have to be shut _down_.

6 VERB PRACTICE *Select the verb that best completes each sentence and write it in the blank space.*

1. The car engine _____ harmful gases.
   a. emitted
   b. discovered
   c. populated

2. Tripping over a rock, Charles _____ and fell down.
   a. slept
   b. stumbled
   c. determined

3. He _____ his car with a pollution-control device.
   a. equipped
   b. reversed
   c. discarded

4. They _____ air pollution but could not eliminate it.
   a. hovered
   b. reduced
   c. strengthened

5. She __wore__ a paper dress once and then threw it away.
   a. stumbled
   b. staggered
   c. wore

6. Americans _____ 48 billion cans last year.
   a. discarded
   b. reversed
   c. restated

7. Engineers _____ scrap metal with cement to make bricks.
   a. lost
   b. mixed
   c. found

8. The workman _____ the toaster.
   a. controlled
   b. concentrated
   c. repaired

9. Air pollution _____ our health.
   a. helps
   b. improves
   c. threatens

10. To control water pollution, cities _____ sewage treatment plants.
   a. built
   b. destroyed
   c. emitted

7 **_SYNONYMS_**   *Rewrite the following sentences, replacing the word or phrase in italics with the best synonym from the list. Do not use any synonym more than once.*

pollution-control device	diapers	"throw-away" technology
wrongdoer	dispose	exhausted
foresight	dilemma	hovers
slogan	crucial	scrap
dump	toothpaste tubes	
	crucial	

1. When we *get rid* of something, we discard it.

When we dispose of some thing, we discard it

2. Our natural resources are being rapidly *used up.*

Our natural resourses are being rapidly exhausted

3. Sometimes we lack *the ability to see into the future.*

Sometimes we lack foresight

4. We must either stop using our cars or suffer air pollution. This *unsatisfactory choice* has no solution.

dilemma

5. Dirty air *floats* over many of our cities.

hovers

6. "Buy now, pay later." This is the *byword* of American business.

slogan

7. *Waste* metal is sold to steel mills.

scrap

8. The *culprit* was given a prison sentence.

wrongdoer

9. The *decisive* moment in the battle was the infantry attack.

crucial

10. Don't *throw* garbage in the water!

dump

8
PREPOSITIONS *Insert the correct preposition in each blank.*

1. Industry sells endless quantities _____ manufactured goods.

2. Many _____ these goods are eventually discarded.

3. _____ all our knowledge, we still lack foresight _____ managing our affairs.

4. Pollutants are dumped _____ the water, _____ the land, and _____ the air.

5. Check _____ defects in the exhaust system _____ your car.

6. Reduce your use _____ electricity and _____ water.

7. Leave your car _____ the garage.

8. The smokestacks _____ buildings should be equipped _____ filters.

9. Instead _____ burning coal, use clean fuels like gas and oil.

10. Go _____ the police _____ reports _____ violations _____ antipollution regulations.

9
WORD-FORM CHART *Study the following words.*

PARTICIPLE	NOUN	VERB	ADJECTIVE	ADVERB
polluted polluting	pollution	pollute		
consumed consuming	consumer consumption	consume		
reduced reducing	reduction	reduce	reducible	reducibly
manufactured manufacturing	manufacturer manufacture	manufacture		

PARTICIPLE	NOUN	VERB	ADJECTIVE	ADVERB
eliminated eliminating	elimination	eliminate		
discarded discarding	discard	discard		
disposed disposing	disposal	dispose	disposable	
	rapidity		rapid	rapidly
	carelessness		careless	carelessly
	greed		greedy	greedily
contaminated contaminating	contamination	contaminate		
related relating	relation relative	relate	relative	relatively
	ingenuity		ingenious	ingeniously
fertilized fertilizing	fertility fertilizer fertilization	fertilize	fertile	
emitted emitting	emission	emit		
concentrated concentrating	concentrate concentration	concentrate		

10 **WORD-FORM EXERCISE**   *In the blank space, insert the correct form of the italicized word.*

1. *consume*   Are you a _Consumer_-oriented person?

2. *concentrate*   The _Concentration_ of pollutants in the air reached a dangerous level yesterday.

3. *contamination*   Do not _Contaminate_ the water supply!

4. *ingenious*   Anne showed her _ingenuity_ in solving the problem.

5. *relate*   Do India and China have diplomatic _relations_?

6. *fertilize*   How much ~~Fertilizer~~ should a farmer use?

7. *emit*   Can we reduce auto ~~emissions~~?

8. *manufacture*   Who ~~manufactured~~ this can opener?

9. *reduction*   This package is too heavy. ~~reduce~~ the weight by removing something.

10. *rapid*   How ~~rapidly~~ can you run around the block?

11. *relation*   ~~relate~~ these ideas and you will have the answer to the problem.

12. *concentration*   ~~Concentrate~~ on the problem and you will find the solution.

13. *ingenuity*   The solution was positively ~~ingenious~~

14. *dispose*   Are you wearing anything that is ~~disposable~~?

15. *contaminate*   Water ~~contamination~~ kills thousands of fish each year.

11 PARTICIPLES   *Insert the correct form of the participle in the blank space.*

1. *pollute*   Do not drink _____ water.

2. *pollute*   DDT is a water-_____ chemical.

3. *manufacture*   How can we dispose of worn-out _____ goods?

4. *manufacture*   This _____ process will increase production.

5. *reduce*   Do you go to a weight-_____ salon?

6. *reduce*   The _____ use of soft coal lowered air pollution.

7. *fertilize*   Crops grow well in _____ fields.

8. *discard*   _____ autos in junkyards surround our cities.

9. *concentrate*   _____ fruit juice mixed with water makes a delicious drink.

10. *eliminate*   Bob was the _____ runner, so he had to drop out of the race.

12 **READING COMPREHENSION** *Choose the wording (a, b, or c) that best completes each sentence. Then rewrite the complete sentence correctly.*

1. We must consume more manufactured goods because this
   a. produces the jobs we need.
   b. surrounds each city with an attractive junkyard.
   c. increases desirable air and water pollution.

2. About 200 years ago, people lived in closer harmony with their environment because
   a. they had no industries.
   b. the junkyards weren't full yet.
   c. their wastes were absorbed by nature.

3. Smog is a form of
   a. water pollution.
   b. air pollution.
   c. land pollution.

4. In a disposable technology like ours, we do the following with a broken toaster:
   a. repair it.
   b. throw it away.
   c. use an alternative source of energy.

5. Women will soon be wearing paper dresses because
   a. they are sexier.
   b. they are more fashionable.
   c. they can be worn once and discarded.

6. We can solve the problem of discarded automobiles by
   a. selling the discards to other countries.
   b. using the scrap metal to make bricks.
   c. building more junkyards.

7. The solution to water pollution is
   a. dumping more sewage in the ocean.
   b. treating the sewage with DDT.
   c. building more sewage-treatment plants.

8. In creating air pollution, the principal wrongdoer is the
   a. automobile.
   b. factory.
   c. apartment building.

9. The best way to eliminate pollution is to
    a. shut down all power plants.
    b. stop running all cars and buses.
    c. employ determined public action.

10. Through the uncontrolled use of insecticides, people have
    a. protected animal life.
    b. polluted the land.
    c. increased the production of paper.

13
WORD PUZZLE: "POLLUTION" *Seventeen key words from this chapter are hidden in the puzzle. How many of the words from the list below the diagram can you find? They read forward, backward, up, or down, are always in a straight line, and never skip letters. Two words—**gas** and **can**—have been circled to get you started. Some letters may be used more than once, and some letters not used at all. Are you a good word detective? Happy hunting.*

```
J  U  N  K  Y  A  R  D  S  O
B  S  E  W  A  G  E  I  M  X
O  L  Q  A  G  A  N  L  O  W
T  U  G  S  R  R  A  E  G  A
T  D  A  T  E  B  T  M  R  T
L  G  S  E  E  A  U  M  X  E
E  E  O  O  D  G  R  A  I  R
S  C  R  A  P  E  E  X  X  C
C  H  E  M  I  C  A  L  Q  A
P  O  L  L  U  T  I  O  N  N
```

air	gas	sewage
bottles	greed	sludge
can	junkyard	smog
chemical	nature	waste
dilemma	pollution	water
garbage	scrap	

14 ***CONTROLLED COMPOSITION***   *Rewrite the selection below. Two ways are provided.*
Follow the directions in each step.

Pollution

¹There is so much natural beauty in the United States—rivers, mountains, plains, farms. ²It is a shame to spoil this scenery with man-made pollution. ³If we are to clean up the environment everybody must help. ⁴The latest idea is an "ecology drive." ⁵Last weekend, as a school project, students in New York, New Jersey, and Connecticut collected discarded bottles and cans, under the leadership of Betty Brown.

⁶BETTY: In our region, we collected more than 100 tons of glass (about 400,000 bottles) and 5 tons of aluminum (about 200,000 cans).

⁷JACK: Students used their cars to transport the junk to collection centers. And they got paid, too.

⁸BETTY: A national soft drink company paid them 21 cents a pound for aluminum cans and 10 cents a pound for bottles.

⁹JACK: Even little kids are helping.

¹⁰BETTY: Yesterday, the average load totaled 70 pounds, and the average payment was $14.70.

¹¹JACK: But not everything can be recycled. The centers don't want cans made of steel, for instance.

¹²BETTY: To be accepted, cans and bottles must be clean.

¹³JACK: The salvaged aluminum is used to make new cans, and the glass is melted down to make new bottles.

¹⁴BETTY: I liked the slogan on a billboard I saw yesterday. It said, "Do Not Litter and Our Town Will Glitter."

1. Rewrite the selection in *direct speech,* keeping each line of dialogue in a separate paragraph. Add necessary punctuation—quotation marks, commas, and phrases such as "Betty said." To add variety, you can use such verbs as "reported," "added," "commented," "asserted," as synonyms for "said." Your second paragraph will begin:

   > Betty said, "In our region, we collected more than 100 tons of glass (about 400,000 bottles) and 5 tons of aluminum (about 200,000 cans)."

2. Rewrite the selection in *reported speech,* making one paragraph out of the conversation. There will be two paragraphs in all. As synonyms for "said," use the verbs suggested in step 1. The second paragraph will begin:

   > Betty said that in her region the students collected more than 100 tons of glass (about 400,000 bottles) and 5 tons of aluminum (about 200,000 cans).

15 TOPICS FOR WRITING AND DISCUSSION

1. Do you have air, land, or water pollution in your country? What steps should be taken to eliminate this problem?
2. Explain what "throw-away" technology is and discuss the good and bad features of this system.
3. The people in a large city have been dumping garbage in the ocean, polluting the air, and contaminating the drinking water. Cans and bottles have piled up, and the city is surrounded by junkyards. Explain the dangers of this situation and tell what the city should do about it.
4. What can you do personally to control pollution?
5. What would you recommend that Americans do to make their country beautiful again? Be specific.

16 DICTATION

1. We live in a throw-away society.
2. We manufacture consumer goods in endless quantities.
3. Where can we throw these disposable products?
4. The junkyards are full of rusting autos.
5. There isn't room for much more waste.
6. People are caught in a vicious cycle.
7. At one time, wastes could be absorbed by nature.
8. We need foresight and planning.
9. We see, smell, taste, and stumble through pollution.
10. Part of the problem is our exploding population.

Twelve

THE AMERICAN INDIANS

A People in Crisis

Indians were the first Americans. They populated North America long before the continent was settled by Europeans. Through a long and difficult struggle that continues to this day, the Indians strove to preserve their traditions, their religion, and their culture. In this they have shown great determination, continuing to hunt and fish or to manage small farms, just as their ancestors did. But compared to other Americans, most Indians are poor. And this is their dilemma. Conditions that favored the old life are gone forever, and yet many Indians are unable to adopt white people's ways. They are alienated, living in the midst of plenty but rejecting efforts that would relieve their poverty at too high a cost to their way of life. In the 1970s, to express their discontent, some Indians "went on the warpath." They shot law officers and committed other acts of violence. This only got them into trouble. More recently, the Indians, whose land claims involve thousands of acres, have asked the courts and the state and federal legislatures for help. We are sure to hear more about these actions in the months ahead. Who are the Indians? Where did they come from? Where do they live today? Above all, why do they feel so mistreated?

(1) The American Indians are of Asian ancestry (distantly related to the Chinese and other Mongolian peoples). Thousands of years before Columbus came to the New World, they entered North America by crossing a narrow strip of land that once connected Alaska and Siberia. Ancient geological changes raised the level of the oceans, covering this natural bridge with water. Today this

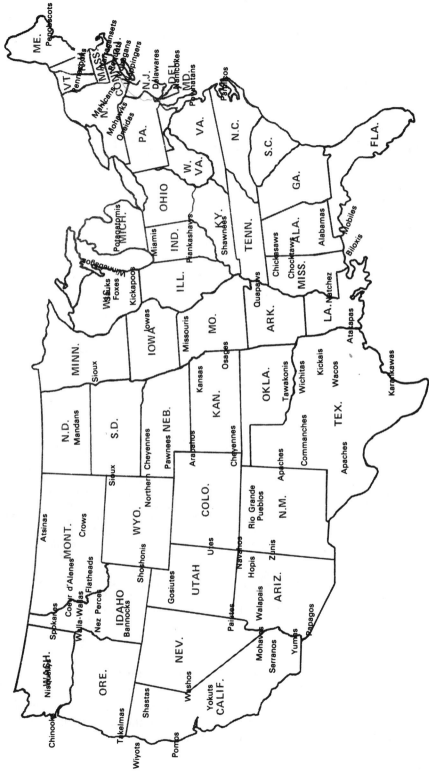

The United States. The principal Indian tribes are shown on this map.

178

place is called the Bering Strait. At its narrowest point, the Strait is only 56 miles wide. In ancient times, as today, a crossing there, even by primitive boat or raft, must have been comparatively easy.

(2)   The migrants entered a new world in which there were no people at all. But there were many animals to hunt, and there were forests where nuts, roots, and berries could be gathered. Living comfortably on this food supply, the newcomers spread out. Some moved south into Central and South America. Others traveled east to the Atlantic Ocean. These migrations were gradual, probably taking thousands of years. Eventually, the people who became the American Indians had spread across North America.

(3)   These migrants contained groups of quite different cultural ancestry. This is evident in the variety of languages they spoke. There are at least 200 separate Indian languages in North America, each with its own grammar and vocabulary. And none is related in any way to English or any other European language.

(4)   The regions of North America where the newcomers lived vary greatly in terms of terrain, climate, and food supply. In adapting themselves to local conditions, the Indians evolved quite different techniques for human survival. In the plains and eastern forests, where game was plentiful, the Indians hunted and fished. In the dry Southwest, they farmed. These regional differences explain the richness and variety of Indian culture: dissimilar economies produced quite different social systems.

(5)   For instance, many Indians of the Southwest, such as the Hopi and the Zuñi, were village Indians. They built mud-brick houses called pueblos and developed agriculture. Many of them learned to irrigate; others became expert dry farmers. They grew beans, corn, and other vegetables. They made baskets, raised and wove cotton, and made beautiful pottery. They made jewelry of turquoise and shell. They danced and sang and worshiped nature gods.

(6)   The Sioux, on the other hand, were Plains Indians. They were nomads who moved from place to place in the area that is now North and South Dakota, Nebraska, and Minnesota. Being great hunters, they were able to kill the buffalo, a large animal that roamed the prairies in vast herds. Killing a buffalo was no easy matter. It took skill and courage. When a herd was sighted, the men, who were called "braves," would creep silently through the tall grass toward an animal on the edge of the herd. Then they would shoot it with their bows and arrows. A safer method often used by the Indians was to drive the herd over a steep cliff. The animals would be killed by the fall. Any survivors would be quickly finished off by the Indian braves at the bottom of the cliff. Then the Sioux would have a great feast. There was plenty of meat for everyone. They made tents, or tepees, from the buffalo skins, and used the hides for clothes and shoes.

(7)   From the European viewpoint, the Indians were a primitive, Stone Age people, who made their tools from stone, bone, horn, or wood. The Indians did not know how to work in bronze or iron. They did no mining or lumbering.

Sometimes Indians drove a buffalo herd over a steep cliff. Any buffalo that survived the fall were killed by other Indians waiting at the bottom.

Their farms, if they had any, were small. And they did not ranch. These were all enterprises that the whites were eager to start . . . but the Indians were in the way. A cultural clash was inevitable.

(*8*) At first, relations were friendly. The Indians taught the settlers how to plant corn, bake clams, make canoes, eat pumpkins and squash, and smoke tobacco. In return, the whites introduced horses, guns, gunpowder, alcohol—and smallpox.

(*9*) As the Europeans established towns and cities, they pushed the Indians back. Sometimes the settlers bought the land from the Indians, usually for a ridiculous price. The Dutch, for example, are supposed to have bought Manhattan Island, the site of present-day New York City, for $24 worth of kettles, axes, and cloth. Sometimes the whites made treaties with the Indians, exchanging one piece of land for another. But in the end, it was the Indians who had to move. Any resistance usually cost them their lives.

(*10*) This struggle for land could have only one result—war. The Indians organized themselves for resistance. Under leaders like Rain-in-the-Face, Sitting Bull, and Red Cloud, they defended their rights and their lands. Sometimes they won battles. One Indian victory long remembered was the massacre of General George A. Custer and 225 men of the U.S. Seventh Cavalry at the Little Bighorn River in Wyoming in 1876. In the end, however, the Indians were defeated.

(*11*) The wars over, the government took steps to end the "Indian problem" for good. All the Indians were moved to large tracts of land called reservations. There they could be policed by the army and administered by a Federal bureau. Today the largest centers of Indian population are Oklahoma, with more than 110,000 Indians; Arizona, with an estimated 75,000; New Mexico, with 50,000; and California, with 25,000. Many other states, such as New York, Connecticut, and Florida, have small communities. Concentrating the Indians on reservations removed them from normal contacts with whites and helped lay the foundations for their later problems.

(*12*) What could the Indians do on these reservations? The old life was over. No longer free to roam the land and hunt the buffalo, nomadic Indians were forced to settle down; farming tribes were often given poor land. How could they earn a living? Barely out of the Stone Age technologically, they did not know how to work for whites, whom they distrusted in any case. And in virtual isolation on their reservations, it was not easy for the Indians to learn new ways or acquire job skills. Nor did their own culture help them adjust. The Indians were used to life in the open. They found white people's everyday, nine-to-five work routine unnatural and restrictive. Coming from an economy in which cash had no place, they were not motivated to accumulate money. Saving today for a useful project in the future was not part of their culture. They spent money as fast as they got it, often on trivial things. As a result, they were always poor and always discouraged. In addition, there was the language problem. The Indians spoke their own language at home. They had to learn English as a second language in school. Many, not understanding the importance of English

These are old-fashioned Indians in a Hollywood movie. The chief is wearing a feathered hat and carrying a peace pipe. Are these Indians progressive enough to fit into modern-day life?

as a work skill, neglected this study. Indians who could not read and write were poorly paid—if they could find work at all.

(*13*) This, briefly, is the background; but what of the Indians today? Some, embittered by past mistreatment, are determined to preserve their tribal life. They insist on their ancestral rights to all lands and all hunting and fishing privileges guaranteed by early treaties. In this attitude they run afoul of the law. For there have been many changes since these treaties were signed. Lands have been leased to ranchers, often by the Indians themselves. In some areas the game and fish are nearly wiped out, and so state and local laws restrict or prohibit hunting and fishing. The Indians reject these laws, which were created by whites and which, they say, do not apply to Indians. The result: friction with the surrounding community and trouble with the FBI.

Some Indians have protested by occupying U.S. Government lands and buildings. But this has gotten them in trouble with the law.

(14) On the other hand, some Indian tribes wish to modernize the reservations. They have set up cattle ranches and started small industries. The value of education is understood, with many Indians of these tribes earning graduate degrees as teachers, doctors, and engineers at their state universities.

(15) These alternatives, with many variations, are what most Indians have chosen—a future in modern technology and education, or the revival of ancient tradition and treaties. One thing is certain—the Indians, with an annual population growth of 4 percent, will not disappear. Hence we cannot ignore their problems. Unfortunately, most Americans do not think of Indians as "modern," but cling to an outmoded picture of the warrior brave as a romantic figure in war paint and a feather bonnet. And this image, entombed in countless novels, magazine stories, and Hollywood movies, hinders Indian advancement. Only when Indians are accepted by Americans as a progressive people will they be free to handle their own affairs and participate fully in our society.

Exercises

1 SCANNING *To do this exercise, glance at the text for information, then, eyes up, give the response.*

1. Who are of Asian ancestry?
2. To whom are the Indians related?
3. When did these Asian people enter the New World?
4. How did the Asians enter the New World?
5. What did a strip of land once connect?
6. What changes raised the level of the oceans?
7. What covered the natural bridge?
8. How wide is the Bering Strait at its narrowest point?
9. What means of transportation did the Asians use to cross the Bering Strait?
10. Who entered the New World?
11. What did the migrants find in the New World?
12. What did they gather?
13. How did the newcomers live?
14. Where did the newcomers go?
15. How long did these migrations take?
16. What kind of ancestry did these migrants have?
17. How do you know?
18. How many separate Indian languages are there?
19. Which of these languages is related to English?
20. In what respects did the regions vary?
21. How did the Indians adapt to local conditions?
22. Where was game plentiful?
23. Where did they farm?
24. What explains the richness of Indian culture?
25. What kind of Indians are the Hopis?
26. What did they build?
27. What did they develop?
28. What did they learn?
29. What did they become?
30. Why did they make?
31. What did they do?

32. Who are the Plains Indians?
33. Who moved from place to place?
34. Which states did they once occupy?
35. Who could kill buffalo?
36. Which animal roamed the prairies?
37. What did killing a buffalo require?
38. What were the Indian men called?
39. How would they approach the herd?
40. What would they shoot with their bows and arrows?
41. What was a safer method?
42. What would be killed by the fall?
43. Who would finish off the survivors?
44. What would the Sioux do then?
45. What did they have for everyone?
46. What did they use the skins for?
47. From what material did the Indians make their tools?
48. Did the Indians use metal?
49. What other European enterprises were the Indians unable to do?
50. What was inevitable?

2 **VOCABULARY DEVELOPMENT**   *Study the following words.*

ancestry	tent	site
geology	cliff	treaty
migrants	creep	bureau
nomads	enterprise	privilege

1. A series of ancestors is one's **ancestry.** "The Smiths are of English and French **ancestry.**"
2. **Geology** is the study of the history of the earth through the analysis of rocks and land formations.
3. **Migrants** move their homes from one place or country to another. A migration is the act of making such a move. "Bird migrations are common in the spring and fall each year."
4. **Nomads** have no permanent home but are always on the move. The Sioux Indians were nomadic because they lived off the buffalo and had to move when the buffalo did.

5. A **tent** is a temporary shelter with a wood or metal frame covered with cloth. The Indians made their tents of buffalo skins and called them **tepees.**

6. A **cliff** is a hill with steep sides.

7. To **creep** is to move on one's hands and knees.

8. An **enterprise** is an undertaking, usually a business of some kind.

9. A **site** is the place where something is located. "How many building **sites** are there on an acre of land?"

10. A **treaty** is an agreement, usually in writing, between people, states, or countries.

11. A **bureau** is a government office or department. The Indians are under the Bureau of Indian Affairs, which belongs to the Department of the Interior. An official who works in a **bureau** is called a bureaucrat.

12. A **privilege** is a right or special permission given a person.

3 **VOCABULARY PRACTICE**   *Fill in the blank spaces, using the vocabulary words above.*

1. The gypsies are __Nomads__ because they have no permanent home.

2. __Migrants__ also move from place to place but have a destination, and, in the case of birds, make the same trip each year.

3. Most modern Italians are of ancient Roman __ancestry__.

4. A baby __creeps__ on the floor.

5. I studied earth history in my __Geology__ class last year.

6. Plains Indians lived in __tent__ made of skins, which they called __tepees__.

7. When hill climbing last summer, I fell off a steep __cliff__.

8. What are the __privilege__ that go with this job?

9. What did the combatants sign at the end of World War II? They signed a peace __treaty__.

10. Shall we start a business __enterprise__?

11. Have you selected a ___site___ for the new office building?

12. Which ___bureau___ in the City Hall do you go to for a marriage license?

4 ***VOCABULARY PRACTICE***   *Circle the letter (a, b, or c) in front of the answer that has the same meaning as the italicized word in the sentence.*

1. A narrow strip of land once *connected* Alaska and Siberia.
   a. joined
   b. separated
   c. hid

2. Indian *migrations* were gradual.
   a. people moving
   b. people hunting
   c. people working

3. The Indians *adapted* to local conditions.
   a. adjusted
   b. discovered
   c. developed

4. Indians in the Southwest built *pueblos*.
   a. mud-brick houses
   b. hunting grounds
   c. farms

5. Buffalo live in *herds*.
   a. domestic animals
   b. single animals
   c. groups of animals

6. The Indian *braves* wore war paint.
   a. the fighting women
   b. the fighting men
   c. the men and women

7. Indian braves wore *war paint*.
   a. paint for the face and body
   b. paint for the pueblo
   c. paint for the clothes.

8. The Indians disliked white people's *routine.*
  a. appearance
  b. daily schedule
  c. education

9. In some areas, the game and fish were nearly *wiped out.*
  a. killed
  b. distributed
  c. reproduced

10. Indians have set up cattle *ranches* in some states.
  a. communities
  b. cities
  c. farms

Exercise 5

SYNONYMS *Rewrite the sentences following, replacing the word or phrase in italics with the best synonym from the word list. Do not use any synonym more than once.*

trivial	alternatives	tracts	primitive
routine	site	barely	tent
roamed	hinders	advancement	terrain
treaty	outmoded	prohibited	buffalo
wiped out	accumulate	restricted	
annual	evolved	nomads	
leased	feast	migrations	

1. The *people with no fixed home* roamed from place to place.
2. Over many thousands of years, animals have *developed* special organs that assist them in adapting to their environment.
3. The *land* of North America is quite varied.
4. Vast *movements* of birds from one place to another occur each year.
5. *Uncivilized* peoples live in the jungles of Central America.
6. Buffalo *wandered around* the prairies in great herds.
7. A *big dinner* is being planned at the Chinese Embassy.
8. When we go camping, we live in a *small, collapsible cloth house.*
9. At the end of World War II, the combatants signed a peace *agreement.*
10. What is the *location* of the new building?
11. This region was divided into large *pieces of land.*
12. Our *regular schedule* leaves little time for entertainment.

13. Some people never *save* any money.

14. They had *hardly* enough time to catch the train.

15. The dog was kept on a leash. His movements were *limited*.

16. The children spent their money on *unimportant* things.

17. The farmer *rented* the land from the government.

18. Possession of firearms is *forbidden*.

19. Some wild birds have almost been *eliminated* in our area.

20. What *options* do you have in making this decision?

6
VERB PRACTICE   *From the list below, select the verb that best completes the meaning of each sentence. Do not use any verb more than once.*

accumulate	leased	prohibited
established	settle	shoot
grow	creep	feel
talk	survive	moved
drive	modernize	survive
rejected	puts	gathered
roam	insist	

1. Antelope _____ the prairies.

2. Farmers _____ corn.

3. Technological inferiority _____ many people at a disadvantage.

4. Do you like to _____ money?

5. The ranchers _____ the land from the Indians.

6. Do you always _____ on your rights?

7. The sign read, "Hunting _____ here."

8. When you get married, you have to _____ down.

9. The Europeans _____ towns and cities.

10. To kill buffalo, you _____ them over a cliff.

11. You can also _____ them with a bow and arrow.

12. The Indians _____ the white man's law.

13. Should we _____ the reservations?

14. To approach a buffalo, you must _____ up on it silently.

15. They _____ nuts, roots, and berries.

7 ***ANTONYMS*** *For each word at the right, find the correct antonym. Write the antonym in the space. Do not use any antonym more than once.*

casualty
escaveal scarce ✓
superior ✓
assist
old-timer
unlimited ✓
noisily ✓
settled people ✓
up-to-date
run ✓
sell
important ✓
language
discard
separate
attack *atacar*
water
wide ✓

1. Important trivial

2. wide narrow

3. attack defend

4. _____ outmoded

5. _____ newcomer

6. _____ hinder *prevenir*

7. run creep

8. Superior inferior

9. Unlimited restricted

10. Settled People nomads

11. _____ gather

12. scarce plentiful

13. separate connect

14. _____ survivor

15. noisily silently

8
PREPOSITIONS   *Insert the correct preposition in each blank space.*

1. Indians work well _____ one another.

2. They hunt _____ food together and help one another _____ an emergency.

3. One hunt, _____ which all the Indians took part, was especially remembered.

4. The Indians sighted a herd _____ buffalo _____ a cliff.

5. The men who were _____ horseback called _____ their wives.

6. "Hide _____ the grass _____ the cliff," they said.

7. "_____ the hunt, we will find you."

8. The braves shot their arrows _____ the buffalo and hit many _____ the side.

9. _____ the hunt, the Indians cut the meat _____ strips and put them _____ a pot to cook.

10. There was plenty _____ meat _____ the pot _____ everyone.

9
WORD-FORM CHART   *Study the following words.*

PARTICIPLE	NOUN	VERB	ADJECTIVE	ADVERB
survived surviving	survival survivor	survive		
varied varying	variety	vary	various	variously
migrated migrating	migrant migration	migrate	migratory	

PARTICIPLE	NOUN	VERB	ADJECTIVE	ADVERB
evolved evolving	evolution	evolve	evolutionary	
connected connecting	connection	connect	connective	connectively
	culture		cultural	culturally
irrigated irrigating	irrigation	irrigate		
organized organizing	organization	organize		
	technology		technological	technologically
restricted restricting	restriction	restrict	restrictive	restrictively
motivated motivating	motivation	motivate		
accumulated accumulating	accumulation	accumulate		
discouraged discouraging	discouragement	discourage		
modernized modernizing	modernization	modernize	modern	
	alternative	alternate	alternative	alternatively

10 WORD-FORM PRACTICE   *In the blank space, insert the correct form of the italicized word.*

1. *survive*   His _____ depended on help from Eileen.

2. *culture*   The French Embassy sponsors many _____ activities.

3. *irrigate*   Farmers use _____ canals to _____ their crops.

4. *technological*   A country needs advanced _____ to launch a space-ship.

5. *accumulate*   There was a steady _____ of rain on the road.

6. *discourage*   Have you had any _____ in your life?

7. *alternate*   Are there any _____ to this plan?

8. *migration*   To breed, many fish and birds always _____ to their breeding grounds.

9. *evolution*   The modern horse _____ from a little animal the size of a dog.

10. *connect*   Plumbers make the pipe _____ in a new building.

11. *survive*   Were there any _____ from that accident?

12. *motivate*   A student needs _____ to learn English.

13. *vary*   "_____ is the spice of life."

14. *technology*   Is Germany a _____ advanced country?

15. *restriction*   The rules in this school are too _____.

11 **PARTICIPLES**   *Insert the correct form of the participle in the blank space.*

1. *restrict*   This is a _____ beach, reserved for village residents.

2. *organize*   Alice has a regular daily routine. She is a well-_____ person.

3. *motivate*   Fred is conscientious. He is a highly _____ student.

4. *motivate*   What is the _____ principle in this work?

5. *accumulate*   It was raining hard. The _____ water half covered the road.

6. *accumulate*   The garbage can was full. The truck took the _____ garbage away.

7. *discourage*   Lois discouraged everybody. She made _____ remarks.

8. *modernize*   The building has been renovated. Now it is a thoroughly _____ school.

9. *modernize*   Frank Lloyd Wright was a _____ influence in architecture.

10. *survive*   The _____ buffalo were quickly killed.

11. *irrigate*   In the Southwest, they farm _____ land.

12. *connect*   The plumber installed the _____ pipe.

13. *evolve*   Science is an _____ body of knowledge.

14. *migrate*   _____ birds fly south for the winter.

15. *vary*   Picasso used _____ techniques in his paintings.

12 **READING COMPREHENSION**   *Chose the wording (a, b, or c) that best completes each sentence. Then rewrite the sentence completely.*

1. The ancestry of the American Indian is
   a. Asian.
   b. African.
   c. European.

2. The Indians originally entered North America by crossing
   a. the Pacific Ocean.
   b. the Atlantic Ocean.
   c. the Bering Strait.

3. The Indians entered a new world that was
   a. already settled by Europeans.
   b. completely uninhabited by other people.
   c. inhabited by primitive people.

4. When settling the country, the Indians moved into
   a. North America only.
   b. North and Central America only.
   c. North, Central, and South America.

5. The American Indians all speak
   a. the same language.
   b. a few languages.
   c. over 200 different languages.

6. To get food, the Plains Indians
   a. hunted.
   b. farmed.
   c. bought their food from Europeans.

7. One Southwest Indian tribe is the
   a. Sioux.
   b. Mohegans.
   c. Hopis.

8. The Sioux were considered nomads because
   a. they established permanent villages.
   b. they moved from place to place.
   c. they developed agriculture.

9. The Indians killed the buffalo with
   a. knives.
   b. clubs.
   c. bows and arrows.

10. The hides of the buffalo were
   a. discarded.
   b. given to the Europeans.
   c. used for clothes and shoes.

11. Technologically, the Indians were
   a. very advanced.
   b. just beyond the Stone Age.
   c. at the same level as whites.

12. At first, relations between the Indians and the Europeans were
   a. friendly.
   b. unfriendly.
   c. hostile.

13. The battle of the Little Bighorn was
   a. a victory for the whites.
   (b) a victory for the Indians.
   c. a draw.

14. The state that has the largest Indian population today is
   a. Florida.
   b. Arizona.
   (c) Oklahoma.

15. The most accurate statement about contemporary Indians is:
   a. All Indians reject modern culture and technology.
   b. All Indians accept modern culture and technology.
   (c) Some Indians preserve a traditional way of life, while others have adopted modern culture and technology.

13

Examen

READING COMPREHENSION   *On the basis of the story, mark each of the following statements T if it is true or F if it is false.*

1. __T__ American Indians are distantly related to the Chinese.

2. __T__ Alaska and Siberia used to be connected by a narrow strip of land.

3. __F__ The Indians found very little food when they first arrived from Asia.

4. __F__ All the Indians were nomads.

5. __F__ Before the Europeans arrived, the Indians used horses for transportation.

6. __F__ Several Indian languages are closely related to English.

7. __F__ When moving from one village to another, the Indians carried their goods in wagons.

8. __F__ All Indians have very similar cultures and traditions.

9. __F__ Killing a buffalo is an easy matter.

10. __F__ The Dutch paid a fair price for Manhattan Island.

11. __F__ The Indians found a rich and happy life on the reservation.

12. __F__ General Custer was a friend of the Indians during the war.

14 *CONTROLLED COMPOSITION* *Rewrite the selection below. Two ways are provided. Follow the directions in each step.*

Early Explorers

[1]Europeans began coming to the New World in the 15th century; after all, Columbus, the first to arrive, made his famous discovery in 1492, one of the most interesting errors in history. [2]Thinking he had found a new route to India, Columbus had actually landed on the shores of a new continent. [3]Other Europeans followed. [4]Of all these early explorers, one of the most colorful was Captain John Smith, an Englishman. [5]He sailed for America in 1606, landed in Virginia, traded with the Indians, and wrote a history of his adventures.

1. Rewrite the passage in your own words, breaking up the long, complex sentences in the paragraph into five, six, or more simpler sentences. You *might* begin as follows:

> Europeans began coming to the New World in the 15th century. Columbus was the first to arrive.

2. Rewrite the passage, combining the simple sentences from step 1 with connecting words such as *and, but, so, or,* and *yet* into a pleasing paragraph.

15 *TOPICS FOR WRITING AND DISCUSSION*

1. Have you ever wanted to live a life of complete freedom? Tell where you would go and what you would do.
2. Does your country have an Indian population? Tell where these people live and describe their culture.
3. Indians have been the subject of countless books and movies. Discuss a fictional treatment of Indians with which you are familiar.
4. Today many American Indians live on reservations. Assume you are in a position to assist these people. What changes in this system would you suggest?

5. The Indians hunted wild game with a bow and arrow. Describe how people hunt in your country.

16 DICTATION

1. Some people in this country are of European ancestry.
2. Geological changes have modified the land.
3. To cross a river, you take the bridge.
4. Have you ever been on a raft?
5. Migrants by the millions have passed through New York City.
6. These newcomers spread all across the country.
7. The Indians gathered nuts, roots, and berries.
8. Does your country vary greatly in terrain?
9. What does a farmer use to irrigate his land?
10. Are there any nomads in your country?
11. The buffalo roamed the prairies in vast herds.
12. Creeping up on a buffalo is hard.
13. Who were the survivors of the accident?
14. What shall we serve at the feast?
15. Do you like to eat pumpkin and squash?

Thirteen

WOMEN'S LIBERATION

"What do the women want?" asked one confused male. We've set them up as wives and mothers, treated them with great respect, even put them on a pedestal. Isn't that enough? Not anymore, it isn't! Many women reject the straitjacket role of childbearing and homemaking, jobs women did not choose for themselves but had imposed on them by a male-dominated society. Not that the role of wife and mother is no longer honorable. It is, and numerous women still find homemaking a satisfying career. But in recent years, many thoughtful women have sought to expand this role. They want absolute equality with men—in marriage, in the workplace, in politics. Shouldn't women receive the same pay as men for the same work, have the same educational opportunities, and be able to rise in any occupation as far as they can? It is no exaggeration to call current changes a social revolution—not only for women but for men, too. And there's much more to come.

(1)   Women's Liberation, or Women's Lib, is the name of a broad-based but informal popular movement. It embraces widely varying organizations, people, and ideas. Some are moderate; some are radical. All are concerned with changing the role of women in contemporary society.

(2)   This movement is not a political party. It is more like a forum or platform from which feminists (supporters of women's rights) speak out on women's issues. In books, articles, lectures, television, feminists attack the time-

In a modern office, women hold top positions of responsibility and power.

less inequities built into a male-dominated social system, and suggest possible remedies.

(3) Such inequities are easy to find, according to these women. One of the most objectionable is the unequal distribution of power throughout the system, especially at the top. Take the U.S. government, for example. Although there have been a few women in Congress, there has never been a woman president: not even a serious contender. A woman was nominated for the vice-presidency in 1984, but did not win the election. Not until President Reagan appointed Sandra Day O'Connor to the Supreme Court did a woman serve on the nation's highest judicial body. Before that time, all nine justices had always been men.

(4) For years, women hoped that a new social order would gradually evolve, especially after they won the right to vote. Even getting this right wasn't easy. It required an amendment to the U.S. Constitution, which wasn't passed until 1920. But change has been painfully slow, obstructed, the women say, by men who are unwilling to share their power, and by the women themselves, who lacked organization and a program of goals. In the 1960s and 1970s women determined to change all this. "Revolution, not evolution" was the new slogan.

(5) The key word is *equality*. In every male-female relationship, must the woman always play the secondary role? The fact is that at birth, apart from

Toys help children learn their role in society. This little boy is building something out of wood with a hammer and nails. How can this help him when he grows up? Would a construction toy help this little girl grow up to be an architect or engineer?

obvious anatomical differences, babies, male and female, are very similar, born with much the same drives, capacities, and potentials. As they grow up, children develop gender identity, special attitudes about themselves. These attitudes are psychological, culturally induced, not natural. For instance, the father who wants his son to take an interest in athletics gives him a bat and ball to play with. To stimulate an interest in science and engineering, the boy gets a microscope or chemistry set. Girls are treated differently. Their toys are dolls and tea sets, and they play "house." Is it any wonder that, when they grow up, men become scientists and the women housewives and mothers, completing as adults a process begun in childhood? This process is called "cultural conditioning." People develop the habit of thinking about themselves in a certain way from the time they were children, and these habits become lifelong. *Planear*

✱ *(6)* *Marriage*   The Women's Liberation movement set out to change this. Through the movement, a program of goals and objectives was set forth. Not all women agree on all points, of course; but there is consensus on most of the following: The family must not take precedence over other things women might do. Women must not be tied to the house. Everyone must be free to experiment with new family styles that permit individuals to develop in their own ways. Equal respect must be given to no-child families, communal living, homosexual unions, and older single women. Such terms as "old maid" and "spinster" are sexist and objectionable. After all, there are no corresponding names for men who never marry.

(7)   All housekeeping chores, such as cooking, cleaning (dusting, vacuuming, laundry), food shopping, diaper changing, and child rearing must be divided equally. Household expenses are also shared. Women may keep their maiden names after marriage, to maintain personal identity.

✱ *(8)* *Children*   Having children must be a free choice for both men and women. Women must have the right to end a pregnancy for any reason. Women who choose not to have children should not lose status.

(9)   The work of raising children must be shared equally by the mother and father. It should not be considered a full-time job for either one. Maternity leave must be given not only to mothers but also to fathers, so that they, too, can stay home from work if the need arises.

(10) *Work*   Jobs must be available to both sexes on the basis of individual ability, without the presumption that one sex is more capable than the other. This means that women will enter many lines of work traditionally open only to men.

TRADITIONAL JOBS	NEW OPPORTUNITIES	NONTRADITIONAL JOBS	
housewife/mother	business manager		carpenter
clerk/typist	upper-level executive	laborer	auto mechanic
secretary	engineer		plumber
nurse	doctor		construction
elementary-school	college professor/		worker
teacher	researcher	police officer	
stewardess	airline pilot	firefighter	
		combat soldier	
		priest/rabbi	

Women are finding new careers as police officers.

(*11*) ***Separation of the Sexes*** Women must not be excluded from clubs, restaurants, social events, or professional gatherings where important business or political affairs are transacted. Men-only meetings have just been one more way to exclude women from the power structure.

(*12*) ***Language*** Women need no longer reveal their marital status by styling themselves "Miss" or "Mrs.," but should adopt the indefinite "Ms.," which is similar to "Mr." for men.

(*13*) The use of male terms to include both sexes, such as "chairman," implies that women are mere substitutes for men, or, what is worse, are attempting to do a "man's job." These sexist words should be replaced by nonsexist, neutral language, for instance:

SEXIST LANGUAGE	NEUTRAL LANGUAGE
chairman	chairperson or chair
policeman	police officer
Congressman	Representative

✳ (*14*) ***Dating*** Women may take the initiative in making dates with men if they wish, taking turns buying movie and theater tickets, picking up dinner checks, and paying other expenses.

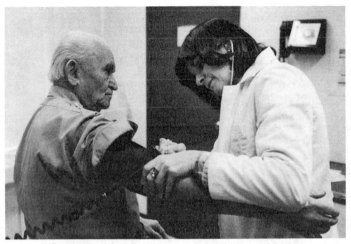

Shouldn't women be doctors as well as nurses?

(*15*)   The Women's Liberation movement has not yet achieved all its goals, some of which are controversial even among women. But the movement has already had considerable impact in many areas of male-female relations. To advance their program, women welcome the cooperation and understanding of men. For the men who are obstinate, unhelpful, and "sexist," women have invented an unpleasant name—male chauvinist pig. And no one wants to be called that!

Exercises

1 SCANNING   *To do this exercise, glance at the text for information, then, eyes up, give the response.*

1. What is the name of a popular women's movement?
2. What kind of ideas does this movement include?
3. Is this movement a political party?
4. If not a party, what is it?
5. What are feminists?
6. What do they do?
7. Where do they express their views?
8. What kind of social system do we have?
9. According to women, what are easy to find?

10. What is one of the most objectionable inequities?
11. Have there ever been any congresswomen?
12. Has there ever been a woman president?
13. Has there ever been a woman vice-president?
14. Who appointed O'Connor to the Supreme Court?
15. When was this done?
16. How many Supreme Court justices are there?
17. What had women hoped would evolve?
18. Did women get the right to vote?
19. When did this happen?
20. Has social change been rapid since then?

2
VOCABULARY DEVELOPMENT *Study the following words. The paragraph from which each word comes is numbered. After studying these words, do exercise 3.*

radical *(1)*	**inequities** *(2)*	**gender identity** *(5)*
role *(1)*	**evolve** *(4)*	**discriminatory** *(12)*
issue *(2)*	**anatomical** *(5)*	**initiative** *(15)*
		controversial *(16)*

1. Political movements are of three broad types: **conservative, moderate,** and **radical. Conservatives** (rightists) usually wish to keep things as they are, unchanged. **Radicals** (leftists) seek sweeping changes, often revolution. **Moderates** (centrists) want something in between, a little change but not a revolution.

2. A **role** is a person's function or duty in society.

   "Betty played the **role** of wife and mother perfectly."

   A **role model** is someone we look up to and imitate, perhaps unconsciously.

   "Martin Luther King is a **role model** for many blacks."

3. An **issue** is a question or matter in dispute, often of public interest.

   "The President spoke out on public **issues** such as unemployment and discrimination."

4. An **inequity** is something unequal and unfair.

5. When something **evolves,** it develops gradually, from one stage to the next.

   "Women hoped political change would **evolve** after they got the vote."

6. **Anatomical** (anatomy). Anatomy refers to the structure of animal bodies, and the study thereof.

> "In **anatomical** detail, the two animals were quite similar."

7. Children develop **gender identity** when they perceive certain activities as "male," other activities as "female," and relate themselves to one of these types.

8. When people are treated unfairly because of race, sex, or religion, this treatment is **discriminatory.**

9. To take the **initiative** is to make the first move, take the first step.

> "Women may take the **initiative** in making dates."

10. A matter is **controversial** when it is unsettled, disputed.

> "Abortion is a **controversial** issue."

③ *VOCABULARY PRACTICE*   *Fill in the blank spaces, using the vocabulary words above.*

1. Jake and Betty were discussing women's rights. At their school, this is a

   topical _issue_, and controversial, too.

2. An action is _discriminatory_ when it is unfair to people because of race, sex, or religion.

3. In politics, people who hold extreme views and want sweeping changes are

   called _radicals_.

4. When something is unequal, it is often unfair. There are many _inequities_ in a male-dominated society, women believe.

5. Betty asked Bill to a movie. She took the _initiative_ in making this date.

6. Men and women are different in _anatomical_ detail, but have many of the same abilities and potentials.

7. Isabel is Catholic. She believes that priests have the right to marry. In her

   church, this is a _controversial_ issue.

8. Sue learned the duties of a housewife by watching her mother, who acted as a ___*role*___ model.

9. When things change slowly, one step at a time, they are said to ___*evolve*___.

10. As a child, Mary played with dolls. Later she learned to sew and cook, because this was what women did, she thought. As an adult, Mary had a strong sense of ___*gender identity*___.

4 SYNONYMS *Rewrite the following sentences, replacing the word or phrase in italics with the best synonym from the word list. Do not use any synonym more than once.*

precedence	tied	stimulate
amended	expecting a baby	diaper
objectives	experiment	obvious
status	microscope	a spinster
chauvinist	contenders	consensus
function	household	allow

1. The Constitution was *changed* to give women the vote. *amended*
2. There are *very clear* differences between moderates and radicals. *obvious*
3. In the early days, women lacked *goals*. *objectives*
4. Mrs. Bell was *an older, unmarried woman*. *a spinster*
5. Women should not lose *social position* if they don't marry. *status*
6. For women, housekeeping should not take *priority* over other things. *precedence*
7. Parents like to *encourage* an interest in science in their children. *stimulate*
8. There is *general agreement* by women on many goals. *consensus*
9. Women should not be *bound and confined* to the house. *tied*
10. Everyone should be free to *try new things*. *experiment*
11. In biology, a *magnifying instrument* is very useful. *microscope*
12. Who are the *competitors* in the election? *contender*
13. What is the *role* of women in society? *function*
14. Some life-styles *permit* a lot of freedom. *allow*
15. Betty is married and *pregnant*. *expecting a baby*

5 SYNONYMS *For each word at the right, find the correct synonym in the list at the left. Write the synonym in the blank space. Do not use any synonym more than once.*

first move
block
disputed *discutir*
strong impression, effect
unhelpful
cure
commercial notice in the
  media
change
meeting
program
keep out — *mantener fuera.*
costs
stubborn — *terco*
unfair treatment
forum
priority
finish

1. _____ *cure* remedy
2. _____ *block* obstruct
3. _____ *meeting* date (with a friend)
4. _____ *finish* complete
5. _____ *costs* expenses
6. _____ *first move* initiative
7. _____ *disputed* controversial
8. _____ *strong impression* impact
9. _____ *keep out* exclude
10. _____ *comercial notice in the media* advertisement
11. _____ *unfair treatment* discrimination
12. _____ *stubborn* obstinate *terco*
13. _____ *change* amendment
14. _____ *priority* precedence

6 ANTONYMS *For each word at the right, find the correct antonym in the list at the left. Write the antonym in the blank space. Do not use any antonym more than once.*

fairness *honesto*
specific
primary
heterosexual
housewife
conservative

1. _____ *conservative* radical
2. _____ *married* single
3. _____ *fairness* inequity

low-cost
conceal
chaotic
role
popular
group
married

4. _conceal_/reveal

5. _primary_ secondary

6. _chaotic_ organized

7. _heterosexual_ homosexual

8. _low-cost_ expensive

9. _group_ individual

10. _specific_ indefinite

7 WORD-FORM CHART   *Study the following words.*

PARTICIPLE	NOUN	VERB	ADJECTIVE	ADVERB
dominated dominating	domination	dominate	dominant	
distributed	distribution	distribute		
appointed	appointment	appoint		
	society	socialize	social	socially
pained	pain		painful	painfully
determined determining	determination	determine	determinable	
evolved evolving	evolution	evolve		
empowering	power	empower	powerful	powerfully
	anatomy		anatomical	anatomically
	culture		cultural	culturally
liberated liberating	liberation	liberate		

PARTICIPLE	NOUN	VERB	ADJECTIVE	ADVERB
respected	respect	respect	respectful	respectfully
	objection	object	objectionable	objectionably
married marrying	marriage	marry	marital	
	controversy		controversial	

(8) **WORD-FORM EXERCISE**   *In the blank space, insert the correct form of the italicized word.*

write on paper

1. *appoint*   The secretary will give you an _____.

2. *evolve*   Darwin discovered the law of _____.

3. *power*   This political party is the most _____ in the country.

4. *anatomical*   Are you taking a class in _____ this semester?

5. *liberate*   The Women's _____ movement is broad-based and popular.

6. *culture*   New York City has many _____ events.

7. *respect*   Bill treated everyone _____.

8. *controversy*   Some of these issues are _____.

9. *pain*   Progress is _____ slow.

10. *anatomy*   The two animals are _____ different.

11. *power*   Are you _____ to make that decision?

12. *domination*   What is the _____ animal in the forest?

13. *marry*   The husband and wife have _____ rights.

14. *society*   Are you on the _____ committee?

15. *objection*   His attitude was _____.   ✓

9 PARTICIPLES   *Insert the correct form of the participle in each blank space.*

1. *liberate*   Are there any _____ women in class?

2. *marry*   The _____ couple took a vacation.

3. *respect*   The doctor was a _____ member of the medical profession.

4. *determination*   What is the _____ factor in this case?

5. *respect*   He holds a highly _____ degree from Harvard University.

6. *appointment*   Please arrive at the _____ time.

7. *pain*   He wore a _____ expression.

8. *power*   Legally, which is the _____ body?

9. *determination*   He had a very _____ look.

10. *evolve*   Knowledge in the field of chemistry is still _____.

10 READING COMPREHENSION   *On the basis of the story, mark each of the following sentences T if it is true or F if it is false.*

1. ____ There are both moderate and radical positions in the women's movement.

2. ____ The movement seeks to improve women's place in society.

3. ____ The movement is a political party.

4. ____ Women use the movement to speak out on issues.

5. ____ Women in the movement favor a male-dominated society.

6. ____ Women want social and political power equally divided.

7. ____ American women won the right to vote in 1901.

8. ____ After women got the vote, social change came quickly.

9. ____ At birth, males and females have comparable drives, capacities, and potentials.

10. ____ Toys help children develop "gender identification," help start the idea that life activities are assigned by sex.

11. ____ According to the movement, men must do their share of the housework.

12. ____ To help with the new baby, fathers must also be given paternity leave from work.

13. ____ Women may hold nontraditional jobs.

14. ____ Women may use Ms. instead of Miss or Mrs.

15. ____ Women may ask men for dates.

16. ____ Women like "sexist" language.

17. ____ According to the movement, women should be allowed to attend men's business and professional meetings.

18. ____ Raising children is the woman's job.

19. ____ A woman qualified in terms of experience and education should be President of the U.S.

11
SKIT *Divide the class into groups. This skit is in two parts, which can be presented by groups working singly or by two groups working together.*

In Part I, have the group assume the traditional male-female roles—the husband as patriarch and wage earner, the wife as mother and homemaker. Other students can play the parts of young people learning to be adults, using their parents as role models. The girls are involved in the mother's work—

cooking, cleaning, sewing, and child care. The boys are involved with the father in outside activities—athletics, a school science project, career planning. All of this can be depicted simply, by showing the family seated in a circle planning for the day ahead, or discussing events in the day just passed. The point to make is that the daily routine of this family has been preset not by each person's interests, abilities, education, or potential, but by sex, with females conditioned to do one thing and males conditioned to do another. This is the way present-day society allocates work, with the limitations obvious and implicit in the system.

In Part II, have the group act out the Liberated World of Tomorrow. As before, the family is seated in a circle, discussing the day's activities. This time, however, equality reigns. The women do the same work as the men, wear the same clothes, call themselves Ms. instead of Miss or Mrs. The older girl is free to ask any boy for a date, pick him up in her car, plan the evening, buy the tickets, pay for dinner, and be responsible for getting him back at the proper time. The mother will have a job as good as or better than her husband's, and will earn as much as or more than he does. He will be heavily involved in the care of the house—spending some time baby-sitting, so that his wife can attend a professional meeting. In this family, roles are interchangeable, not determined by sex. The boys do the cooking; the girls are part-time carpenters, fix the plumbing, and so on. The skit could be further developed on these lines.

After the skit, have the class compare the two versions of society, and discuss the merits and disadvantages of each.

12 GAMES   *For review practice turn to a game in the appendix.*

13 CONTROLLED COMPOSITION   *Rewrite the selection below. Two ways are provided. Follow the directions in each step.*

Liberation

[1]In the past, women were not liberated. [2]They were not frequently given upper-level jobs. [3]They did not always receive equal pay for equal work. [4]They were not elected to presidential office. [5]Women were not free to experiment with new family arrangements. [6]They did not hold nontraditional jobs. [7]They did not use the gender-neutral title Ms. [8]They did not share the care of children with the men. [9]In the past, their lives were not fulfilling.

1. Rewrite the passage. Change "women" to "the average woman" wherever it appears. This means you will be writing about one woman instead of many, so make the verbs and pronouns singular, to agree in number. Your first sentence will say:

In the past, the average woman was not liberated.

2. Pretend the action in the paragraph is happening in the future. Rewrite the passage, changing each sentence from the past tense negative to the future tense affirmative. In sentences 1 and 9, change "In the past" to "In the future." Your first sentence will say:

In the future, women will be liberated.

14 *TOPICS FOR WRITING AND DISCUSSION*

1. The Women's Liberation movement is controversial, even among women. Discuss the pros and cons of this approach to social change.
2. Tell about the role of women in your country. Discuss their present-day status in such areas as work, marriage, education, religion, and politics.
3. In your country, do women aspire to a different way of life? Discuss the changes women would like to make in their life-styles.
4. Would the goals of the Women's Liberation movement work in your country? Give your reasons.
5. Describe a famous woman from your country and tell why you admire her.

15 *DICTATION*

1. Women's Liberation is a popular movement.
2. It contains moderate and radical ideas.
3. There are many inequities in our social system.
4. Power is distributed unequally.
5. The Constitution was amended in 1920.
6. "Revolution, not evolution" is the new slogan.
7. The key word is equality.
8. Women must not be confined to the house.
9. Housework must be shared.
10. Women may take the initiative.

Fourteen

OUR DISAPPEARING WILDLIFE

Wild animals used to roam the United States in uncounted numbers. Today these animal populations have sadly dwindled. Some animals have disappeared altogether, destroyed by the advance of civilization. The same story can be told in Africa, once covered with big game such as elephants, rhinoceros, and antelope. In Central and South America, where animals were once thought safe, they are now threatened. In the last three centuries, more than 200 species of mammals, birds, and reptiles have become extinct. Eight hundred more species are endangered. The endangered species include the gorilla, the orangutan, the giant tortoise, the trumpeter swan, the whooping crane, the big cats, and the whales. Our wild animals are being swept from the land, the birds from the air, the fish from the sea. Romain Gary, a well-known writer on conservation, said, "It may be that man's greatest 'achievement' in the 20th century is not that he traveled to the moon but that he destroyed forever an irreplaceable heritage of natural things."

(1)   Animal life first appeared on the earth about 400 million years ago. Through the passing millennia, thousands of animal species have come and gone. Until recently, this process was gradual, the result of changes in climate, in habitat, or in the genes of the animals themselves. But the tremendous expansion of modern civilization now threatens to upset this natural balance, putting unprecedented pressure on the survival of our wildlife.

(2)   This imbalance can be traced to many causes. Most arise in the greed

Every animal, including the mountain lion, has a useful place in nature.

and poor planning of people. With each increase in our population, the wilderness areas where the animals live get smaller. The use of pesticides to control injurious insects also harms wild birds and animals. Water pollution kills fish in our rivers, lakes, and oceans. Hunters have almost exterminated many of the larger animals like the bighorn sheep and the grizzly bear. And farmers destroy smaller animals like the prairie dog and the coyote. As a result of this unrelenting pressure, our wildlife is disappearing at the rate of one species or subspecies per year.

(3)   Of all the continents, the most drastic reduction in wildlife has occurred in North America, where the transition from a rural to a highly industrialized society has been most rapid. Among the victims are birds, mammals, and fish. We will never again see the passenger pigeon or the eastern elk. They have been wiped out. Of many other species, only a few representatives still survive in the wild. The U.S. Department of the Interior has put no fewer than 109 species on the endangered species list. (An endangered species is one with poor prospects for survival and in need of protection.) This list includes everything from the timber wolf to the whooping crane. Even the bald eagle, our national symbol, is threatened. (amenazada)

(4)   Animals that kill other game for food are called predators. The predators include the wolf, mountain lion, fox, bobcat, and bear. Attack against these animals began with the arrival of the first European settlers, who wished to protect their livestock. Eventually, a reward was offered to hunters for every predator that was killed. This reward is called a bounty. Ironically, the Federal government is the chief funder of predator-control programs.

(5)   The settlers also brought in their Old World fears and superstitions concerning predators. Whether preying on livestock or not, predators were shot on sight. This attitude continues to this day for coyotes, eagles, foxes, mountain lions, and bobcats, and is largely responsible for placing the eastern timber wolf, grizzly bear, and bald eagle on the endangered species list.

(6)   Yet every animal, including the predator, has its place in nature's grand design. Predators help maintain the health of their prey species by eliminating the diseased, young, old, and injured. Predators like the mountain lion and the wolf help to keep the deer herds healthy. Their kill also provides food for scavengers that feed on carrion. Occasional loss of livestock must be weighed against the good these animals do in maintaining the balance of nature.

(7)   The mountain lion has especially suffered from trapping and hunting. This great cat had the widest distribution of any mammal in the Western Hemisphere. Its range extended from northern British Columbia to the tip of South America, and from the Atlantic to the Pacific. But by the turn of the 19th century, this splendid animal was almost extinct in the eastern United States. In the West, the pattern of persecution was similar to that suffered by other predators. As the sheep and cattle empires grew, so did the war on the mountain lion.

(8)   Overhunting an animal is an obvious form of extermination, but there are more subtle processes that often have the same fatal result. One of these is

Can you imagine anyone killing this little seal to make a coat out of its fur?

destruction of habitat. When farmers introduced sheep and cattle to North America, the domestic animals competed with the wild animals for the available grazing land. Animals like the buffalo and the pronghorn antelope, which once roamed the plains in countless numbers, were either killed or pushed off the grasslands. Today, a few remnants of these giant herds are protected from hunters in national game preserves and wildlife refuges.

(9)   Pesticides have also taken their toll. In 1947 a new chemical poison called DDT was introduced. It proved very effective in controlling insect pests like the potato beetle and the boll weevil. But pesticides, which decompose very slowly, accumulate in animals which feed on pest insects or their predators, and the accumulated poisons attack their nervous systems. Pesticides also interfere with the formation of calcium in birds, which then lay eggs with very thin shells or no shell at all. When wildlife fail to reproduce, it isn't very long before they disappear. The bald eagle, 12 species of hawks, and the pelican have been seriously reduced by chemicals.

(10)   Why should we care about the extinction of these birds and animals? The answer is simple enough. Every species that becomes extinct is gone forever. With each departure a small part of the diversity of nature that makes life so interesting is also gone. What has man got to look forward to—endless cities and houses and roads that cross barren country devoid of birds and animals? Is that the world we want for ourselves and our children?

Exercises

1 **SCANNING**   *To do this exercise, glance at the text for information, then, eyes up, give the response.*

1. When did animal life first appear on the earth?
2. What has happened to thousands of animal species?
3. Why did this happen to the animals? Give three reasons.
4. What threatens to upset the natural balance?
5. What part do we play in creating this imbalance? Give four causes that can be traced to humans.
6. On which continent has the most drastic reduction in wildlife occurred?
7. Why did this happen?
8. Which animals have been affected?
9. Which creatures are gone for good?
10. How many species are on the endangered species list?
11. Who says so?
12. Give three examples of animals on this list.
13. What are animals that kill other game called?
14. Give three examples of predators.
15. When did attacks against these animals begin?
16. What is a bounty?
17. Who is the chief funder of bounty programs?
18. What else did the settlers bring in?
19. What was shot on sight?
20. What has its place in nature's design?
21. How do predators maintain the health of their prey species?
22. Which predators keep the deer herd healthy?
23. What does their kill provide?
24. What must occasional loss of livestock be weighed against?
25. Which animal has especially suffered from trapping and hunting?
26. What was the range of this great cat?
27. When did it almost become extinct?
28. Give one subtle process that often leads to extermination.
29. Which animals competed with wild animals for habitat?
30. Where do a few remnants of the giant herds live today?

2 *VOCABULARY DEVELOPMENT* *Study the following words. The paragraph from which each word comes is numbered. After studying these words, do exercise 3.*

extinct (*introduction*)	**predator** (*4*)	**superstition** (*5*)
species (*1*)	**bounty** (*4*)	**scavenger** (*6*)
habitat (*1*)	**prey** (*5*)	**carrion** (*6*)
wilderness (*2*)		

1. An animal becomes **extinct** when all the members of its biological group are dead. The passenger pigeon became **extinct** in 1914, when the last known specimen died in a zoo."

2. A **species** is a biological classification or group of individuals that resemble one another and are able to breed among themselves. "Lions, tigers, and leopards belong to three different **species** within the cat family."

3. Wild animals are always found in an area where the climate, topography, and food supply are favorable to them. This area is their **habitat.** The prairie dog needs soft earth to burrow in and grass to eat, so it is found on the plains or prairie. The horned lizard likes a hot, dry climate and insects to eat, so its **habitat** is the desert.

4. A region that is completely undeveloped, that has no houses or roads and is uninhabited by people, is called a **wilderness.**

5. **Predators** are meat-eating animals such as the mountain lion, wolf, and bob-cat. The animals they kill for food, such as deer and antelope, are called their **prey.** When these animals are hard to find, **predators** will attack domestic animals, such as sheep or cows. Naturally, these attacks annoy farmers and ranchers, who offer a **bounty,** or cash payment, to hunters for each **predator** that is killed.

6. A **superstition** is a false belief not based on scientific knowledge.

7. **Scavengers** are the birds and animals that keep the wilderness clean. After a predator has left its kill, **scavengers** arrive to eat the remaining scraps, or **carrion,** until nothing is left. The vulture is the most famous **scavenger** of all.

Vulture

3 *VOCABULARY PRACTICE* *Fill in the blank spaces, using the vocabulary words above.*

1. Birds such as the vulture that eat the remains of dead animals are called

scavenger

2. Meat-eating animals such as the mountain lion and wolf are called

~~_Predators_~~

3. When a wolf attacks domestic animals, the farmer will offer a _bounty_ to hunters for its destruction.

4. A _habitat_ is an area favorable to specific animals in climate and food supply.

5. When a natural area is completely undeveloped, it is called a _wilderness_ area.

6. The remains of a dead animal that is eaten by scavengers is called

carrion

7. A belief not based on scientific fact is a _superstistion_.

8. The animals that predators attack are called _prey_.

9. When all the members of an animal group die, we say that animal is

extinct

10. A group of animals with the same characteristics belong to the same

species   _pertenece._

_4_
NORTH AMERICAN BIRDS AND ANIMALS   A.   _Here is a list of the animals and birds mentioned in this article. Familiarize yourself with this list._

Wild Mammals
    Predators: meat-eating or carnivorous animals
        grizzly bear
        mountain lion
        fox
        bobcat
        wolf
        coyote

Prey for the predators: grass-eating or herbivorous animals
  elk
  buffalo
  deer
  antelope
  bighorn sheep
Birds
  passenger pigeon
  whooping crane
  bald eagle
  hawk
  pelican
Domestic livestock
  sheep
  goats
  cattle
  poultry

B. *Oral Practice*

1. From the list, name two animals that are prey for the mountain lion.
2. Name two herbivorous animals.
3. Name two carnivorous animals.
4. Name two *large* predators.
5. Name two *small* predators.
6. Which bird is the national symbol of the United States?
7. Among the following animals, which would you prefer as a pet: grizzly bear, wolf, bison, prairie dog, hawk, goat or chicken? Give reasons for your choice.
8. If you were hiking in a wilderness area, which animal would you *least* like to meet on a trail? Explain why.

5

ANTONYMS   *For each word at the right, find the correct antonym in the list at the left. Write the antonym in the blank space. Do not use any antonym more than once.*

protect
obvious   **1.** _____ expand
passive
fertile   **2.** _____ drastic
allow
habitat   **3.** _____ domestic

genes
wild
contract
moderate
cycle
transition
final
millennia
heal
insufficient

4. _____ abundant

5. _____ injure

6. _____ initial

7. _____ subtle

8. _____ active

9. _____ barren

10. _____ ban

11. _____ endanger

6 **SYNONYMS**   *Rewrite the sentences following, replacing the word or phrase in italics with the best synonym from the word list. Do not use any synonym more than once.*

hordes	imminent	carnivorous
habitat	bounties	wiped out
roam	millennia	decompose
animals used for food	threat	carrion
transition	accumulate	grass-eating
species	mountain lion	unrelenting
susceptibility	drastic	

1. Some birds have been *destroyed* by pesticides.

2. The earth has already lasted for *thousands of years.*

3. We must take *very strong* measures to preserve our wildlife.

4. All animals have a *particular place* where they live.

5. The buffalo used to *wander* the prairies by the millions.

6. Predators are less of a *danger* than farmers think.

7. Some *classifications* of animals have disappeared.

8. *Rewards* are paid to hunters who kill predators.

9. Scavengers feed on *dead animals*.

10. Some pesticides do not *disintegrate*.

11. *Meat-eating* animals must hunt their prey.

12. Meat-eating animals must hunt their *prey*.

13. The *change* to an industrialized society was rapid in America.

14. The pressure on our wildlife is *unceasing*.

15. *Herbivorous* animals live on the plains.

7 WORD-FORM CHART   *Study the following words.*

PARTICIPLE	NOUN	VERB	ADJECTIVE	ADVERB
injured injuring	injury	injure	injurious	injuriously
	abundance		abundant	abundantly
expanded expanding	expansion	expand	expansive	expansively
polluted polluting	pollution	pollute		
industrialized industrializing	industry	industrialize	industrial	industrially
	superstition		superstitious	superstitiously
persecuted persecuting	persecution	persecute		
endangered endangering	danger	endanger	dangerous	dangerously
competed competing	competition	compete	competitive	competitively
	susceptibility		susceptible	susceptibly
decomposed decomposing	decomposition	decompose		
accumulated accumulating	accumulation	accumulate		
applied applying	application	apply	applicable	

8 **WORD-FORM PRACTICE**   *In the blank space, write the correct form of the italicized word.*

1. *pollute*   Water _____ is ruining our lakes and rivers.

2. *injure*   The man who had the auto accident received a bad

_____.

3. *superstition*   Are you _____?

4. *application*   _____ this medicine to the cut once a day.

5. *abundance*   There used to be _____ wildlife in the U.S.

6. *decomposition*   Carrion will _____ rapidly in the hot sun.

7. *accumulate*   An _____ of money should be kept in the bank.

8. *competition*   Athletes _____ every four years at the Olympic Games.

9. *danger*   Do you have to live _____ to have fun?

10. *persecution*   Landlords should never _____ their tenants.

11. *danger*   I promise not to _____ your life in my car.

12. *susceptibility*   Are you _____ to disease?

13. *expansion*   He spoke _____ about his many projects.

14. *injure*   DDT is _____ to many birds and animals.

15. *pollution*   Do not _____ the environment.

16. *industry*   The U.S. began to be _____ in the 19th century.

17. *expansion*   You can _____ your knowledge by going to school.

18. *industrialize*   A country needs heavy _____ to manufacture automobiles.

19. *decompose* _____ set in immediately after death.

20. *apply* Jack sent in an _____ for a new job.

9
PARTICIPLES *Write the correct form of the participle in the blank space.*

1. *endanger* Wolves are an _____ species.

2. *pollute* Never drink _____ water.

3. *industrialize* Japan has a heavily _____ economy.

4. *decompose* The _____ zebra lay on the ground, killed yesterday by the lion.

5. *decompose* The _____ zebra, killed six weeks ago by the lion, had completely disappeared.

6. *apply* Ecology is an _____ science.

7. *accumulate* The garbage had fully _____, so they threw it out.

8. *accumulate* The garbage was still _____. They would throw it out tomorrow.

9. *injure* He wore an _____ look when his girl friend told him to "get lost."

10. *expand* After he graduated from college, Herb felt he had acquired newly _____ knowledge.

10
write on paper only answer

READING COMPREHENSION *On the basis of the story, mark each of the following sentences T if it is true or F if it is false.*

1. _F_ The prairie dog is a predatory animal.

2. _F_ The wolf is an extinct animal.

3. _T_ The bald eagle is an endangered species.

4. __F__ The gorilla is closely related to the giant tortoise.

5. __F__ Pesticides that kill injurious insects are beneficial to wildlife.

6. __F__ You are likely to see a passenger pigeon in a city park.

7. __F__ Animals that kill other animals for food are called herbivores.

8. __F__ The wolf serves no useful purpose in nature.

9. __F__ The animal that used to have the widest distribution in the Western Hemisphere was the bear.

10. __F__ DDT increases calcium production in wild birds.

(11) **READING COMPREHENSION** *Choose the wording (a, b, or c) that best completes each sentence. Then rewrite the sentence completely.*

write on paper only answer

1. The mountain lion
   (a.) used to have a wide distribution.
   b. became extinct in the 19th century.
   c. lives mainly on sheep and cattle.

2. Bounty hunters are people who
   a. preserve our wildlife.
   (b.) kill predators for money.
   c. take care of wilderness areas.

3. DDT is a
   (a.) pesticide.
   b. vitamin.
   c. water additive.

4. Predators are
   a. herbivorous animals.
   b. prey animals.
   (c.) carnivorous animals.

5. A scavenger is an animal that
  a. feeds on carrion.
  b. avoids extermination.
  c. attacks livestock.

6. The buffalo is an animal that
  a. was never plentiful.
  b. was once plentiful but is now extinct.
  c. is protected by the federal government.

7. The boll weevil is
  a. a predator.
  b. an endangered species.
  c. an injurious insect.

8. Animal life has been on earth about
  a. 250 million years.
  b. 560 million years.
  c. 400 million years.

9. If we do not protect our wildlife, the earth will soon be
  a. overcrowded with animals.
  b. devoid of animals.
  c. consumed by animals.

10. The bald eagle, the timber wolf, and the whooping crane have one characteristic in common. They
  a. belong to the same species.
  b. are on the endangered species list.
  c. pursue the same prey.

12 **WORD PUZZLE: "WILD BIRDS AND ANIMALS"**   *The names of 20 common birds and animals are hidden in the puzzle. How many names from the list below the diagram can you find? They read forward, backward, up, or down, are always in a straight line, and never skip letters. Two words—***buffalo** *and* **hawk***—have been circled to get you* *started. Some letters may be used more than once, and some letters not used at all. Are you a good word detective? Happy hunting.*

B	U	F	F	A	L	O	W	F	H
B	O	B	C	A	T	W	O	O	A
E	L	K	R	R	X	L	L	X	W
A	N	L	I	O	N	E	F	E	K
V	S	N	A	K	E	O	D	T	S
E	A	G	L	E	X	P	E	O	K
R	B	E	A	R	G	A	E	Y	U
P	I	G	E	O	N	R	R	O	N
D	R	O	B	I	N	D	U	C	K
A	N	T	E	L	O	P	E	O	X

antelope	duck	lion
bear	eagle	owl
beaver	snake	pigeon
bobcat	elk	robin
buffalo	fox	skunk
coyote	hawk	wolf
deer	leopard	

13 *DEBATE: WILDLIFE CONSERVATION AND MANAGEMENT* Divide the class into groups for a debate on the topic, "Wildlife is valuable to people." Have each group organize itself into two teams, one team supporting the topic, the other team opposing it. Each side should think through its arguments carefully. The "pro" side might ask the class to imagine a colorless world devoid of wildlife, and mention the constructive use of animals for food and clothing. The "con" side might mention the cost of maintaining wildlife sanctuaries, and the competition by people for farmland, forests, and so on. Students can give examples of wildlife management from their own countries for additional evidence.

Have the teams debate (quietly) in the corners of the room, with the teacher as mobile observer. The most interesting debate can be repeated for the class as a whole, followed by general discussion.

14 ***CONTROLLED COMPOSITION*** *Rewrite the selection below. Follow the directions in each step.*

The Law of the Jungle

[1]Animals kill animals to live. [2]This is the law of the jungle. [3]It helps keep all wildlife strong. [4]Only vigorous animals escape being eaten. [5]Predators catch the old, the sick, and, sometimes, the young. [6]But this keeps the prey animal from growing too large in number. [7]When the predator is injured or old, it dies of age and hunger. [8]Nature is cruel, but nature loves a balance.

1. Rewrite the passage. Make it more interesting by adding adjectives and adverbs from the reading.
2. Have students put their compositions on the blackboard. Discuss the choice of words that were used or might have been used.

15 ***TOPICS FOR WRITING AND DISCUSSION***

1. What is causing wildlife to disappear? Tell what should be done to correct this situation.
2. Describe the most interesting bird or animal in your country.
3. Imagine that a large dam or lumber operation is to be constructed near a wilderness area. Power from the dam and lumber from the mill are needed by modern industry, so this construction cannot be stopped. What steps would you take to protect the wildlife in that area?
4. Are there any endangered species in your country? Describe their habitat and tell what is being done to preserve them.
5. Write a description of a wilderness area in your country.
6. Tell about a camping trip you took.
7. Do you think hunting and fishing should be prohibited? Explain why you think so.
8. Have you ever visited a zoo? Explain what you saw there.

16 ***DICTATION***

1. The timber wolf is a predatory animal.
2. Wilderness areas are getting smaller.
3. Pesticides control injurious insects.

4. Trapping takes a heavy toll on wildlife.
5. So does the destruction of habitat.
6. Is the bald eagle an endangered species?
7. Is the mountain lion a bounty animal?
8. Are elk and sheep grazing animals?
9. Susceptibility to disease has hurt some big game animals.
10. We must preserve the diversity of nature.

Fifteen

THE OCEANS

Man's Last Great Resource

By the year 2006, the world population will double in size, according to present-day estimates. How will we feed all these people? Most of our food-producing land is already in use. Where will we get minerals and other natural resources to run our industries? The answer is simple. We will be fed, clothed, supplied, maybe even housed, by the world's last great resource—the ocean.

That the oceans should have such untapped potential is not surprising. In size alone they occupy 71 percent of the earth's surface, about 140 million square miles, and contain enough water to cover the earth to a depth of two miles, if the land were smooth and level. From this vast body of water we have always obtained food. Now we get oil there and may eventually get many other resources, too. We may even *live* in the ocean, if pollution and overpopulation make the land uninhabitable.

These changes involve not only technology but also international law, the dual concern of the article that follows by Claiborne Pell, United States Senator from Rhode Island.

(1)   For millennia people have exploited and often destroyed the riches of the land. Now they covet the wealth of the oceans, which cover nearly three-quarters of the earth. But the scramble for minerals and oil, for new underwater empires, could heighten international tensions and set a new and wider stage for world conflict.

(2)   Even the most conservative estimates of resources in the seabed stag-

The oceans are an important source of food.

ger the imagination. In the millions of miles of ocean that touch a hundred nations live four out of five living things on earth. In the seabed, minerals and oil have been proved to exist in lavish supply. The oceans are a source of pure water and food protein; of drugs and building materials; they are even possibly a human habitat, a key to survival for the doubling population on the land.

(3)   People may yet learn to use a tiny fraction of this wealth. Unless international law soon determines how it shall be shared, that fraction alone could set off a new age of colonial war. Is the deep seabed, like the high seas, common to all? Or, like the wilderness areas of land, is it open to national claim by the use and occupation of the first or the strongest pioneer? The question of what is to be done to regulate and control exploitation of the seabeds is no longer a theoretical matter. It is a problem of international concern. We must decide how to divide this great wealth equitably among nations. But wealth is not the only thing at stake. We must also learn how to protect the oceans from the menace of pollution.

(4)   A few years ago, "practical" people dismissed speculations about wealth in the sea. "That is economic foolishness," they said. It will never be economically profitable to exploit the seabeds, no matter how great the riches to be found there. Unfortunately, they underestimated the lure of gold as the mother of invention. Yet the pessimists may be proved right. In these pioneer years of the Ocean Age, the damage done sometimes seems to exceed the benefit gained. Beaches from England to Puerto Rico to California have been soaked in oily slime. Fish and wildlife have been destroyed. Insecticides, seeping into the rivers and then the oceans, have killed fish and waterfowl and revived fears that other lethal chemicals may contaminate our waters when they are used as garbage dumps. The future disposal of increasing amounts of atomic waste is an unresolved problem. Millions of acres of offshore seabed have been leased for drilling. Largely in ignorance, we are tinkering with our greatest source of life.

(5)   The incredible magnitude of the oceans' resources can be measured by just one isolated example: the metal content of manganese nodules. These lumps of mineral on the ocean floor were once regarded as a curiosity with no economic value. One study of reserves in the Pacific Ocean alone came up with an estimate that the nodules contained 358 billion tons of manganese, equivalent, at present rates of consumption, to reserves for 400,000 years, compared to known land reserves of only 100 years. The nodules contain equally staggering amounts of aluminum, nickel, cobalt, and other metals. Most of these resources exist at great depths, from 5,000 to more than 15,000 feet below sea level. Yet within five to ten years the technology will exist for commercial mining operations. This will make available virtually unlimited metal reserves.

(6)   More familiar to most of us is the accelerated pace of offshore drilling that now extends more than 50 miles out to sea and accounts for 15 percent of U.S. oil production. In the twelve years between 1955 and 1967, offshore production of crude oil increased from seven million to 222 million barrels. Estimates of known reserves of natural gas have more than tripled in the past 15 years, and each advance of scientific exploration of the ocean beds brings to light

Scientists conduct research on the ocean floor.

new finds that would gladden the eye of the most hardened veteran of the California gold rush.

(7) Perhaps the least developed resource, and one of critical importance to spiraling population figures, is the use of the seas for farming techniques or "aquaculture." Present methods of fishing can only be compared with primitive

hunting with a bow and arrow; if fish were cultivated like livestock, the present world fish catch could easily be multiplied five- or as much as tenfold. The production of protein concentrate and the distillation of fresh water are still experimental in an economic sense; there is no reason to believe that they too cannot become both useful and profitable. Aquaculture could also be applied to a variety of marine plant life.

(8)   Nor is the potential confined to what we can extract from the seas or the seabed. In crowded England, serious plans have been developed to build entire cities just off the coast. Offshore airports may solve the demand for large tracts of jet-age space near such large coastal cities as New York and Los Angeles. Some people, quick to take advantage of the legal confusion that reigns beyond coastal waters, have planned to build independent islands atop seamounts and reefs outside the country's territorial limit—this is indeed a romantic notion, but one with, it is suspected, the more prosaic aim of avoiding the constrictions of domestic law concerning gambling and taxes. One such venture has been re-strained by the courts on the grounds that the reefs and seamounts attach to the seabed on the continental shelf, and are, therefore, under U.S. jurisdiction. In another case the United Nations was presented with an application for permis-sion to extract minerals from the bed of the Red Sea in an area 50 miles from the coastal states. The Secretariat dodged this thorny question, citing lack of authori-ty to act.

(9)   Such claims are no longer isolated or frivolous. How to dispose of this wealth and exploit these possibilities has become a world problem.

Exercises

1
SCANNING   *To do this exercise, glance at the text for information, then, eyes up, give the response.*

1. How long have people exploited the riches of the land?
2. What do they covet now?
3. What is one factor that could heighten international tensions?
4. What staggers the imagination?
5. What is the percentage of living things that live in the ocean?
6. What can be found in the seabed?
7. What else are the oceans useful for?
8. How much of this wealth may we yet learn to use?
9. What must we consider in determining how the oceans will be used?
10. What else is at stake?

11. "Practical" people used to dismiss speculations about wealth in the sea. How long ago was that?
12. What did they say?
13. What did they underestimate?
14. Who may be proved right?
15. Where have the beaches been soaked in oil?
16. What has been destroyed by the oil pollution?
17. What else may contaminate our waters?
18. How many acres of offshore seabed have been leased for drilling?
19. With what are we tinkering, largely in ignorance?
20. Give one example that shows the magnitude of the oceans' resources.
21. Where are manganese nodules found?
22. How many tons of manganese may be in the Pacific Ocean alone?
23. At present rates of consumption, how long might these reserves last?
24. What other metals are found in the nodules?
25. At what depths are these nodules found?

2 VOCABULARY DEVELOPMENT

Study the following words. The paragraph from which each word comes is numbered. After studying these words, do exercise 3.

exploit (*1*)	**slime** (*4*)	**aquaculture** (*7*)
covet (*1*)	**lethal** (*4*)	**offshore** (*8*)
seabed (*2*)	**incredible** (*5*)	**prosaic** (*8*)
lavish (*2*)	**magnitude** (*5*)	**continental shelf** (*8*)
menace (*3*)	**nodule** (*5*)	

1. To **exploit** something is to use it for your advantage or profit.
2. To **covet** is to desire something. "Do not **covet** your neighbor's wife."
3. The **seabed** is the floor of the ocean.
4. **Lavish** means extravagant or profusely generous. "Bill gave his friends **lavish** gifts."
5. A **menace** is a danger. "Air pollution is a **menace** to our health."
6. **Slime** is a thick, sticky substance that is offensive or disagreeable. "An oil spill left oily **slime** on the beach."
7. **Lethal** means deadly. "Mrs. Jones died from a **lethal** dose of poison."

8. Something **incredible** is unbelievable or seemingly impossible. "A race horse can run at an **incredible** speed."

9. **Magnitude** means great size or amount. "She was impressed by the **magnitude** of his generosity."

10. A **nodule** is a small rounded mass or lump. "Manganese **nodules** lay in abundance on the ocean floor."

11. **Aquaculture** is underwater agriculture, the cultivation of fish and plants in a controlled environment.

12. **Offshore** refers to that part of the ocean some distance from the shore. "**Offshore** drilling produces many oil wells."

13. **Prosaic** means ordinary, commonplace, down-to-earth. "The U.N. has high ideals, but its work is often **prosaic**."

14. The **continental shelf** is a relatively shallow undersea ledge attached to the land and extending out to sea. Good fishing is usually found in this part of the ocean.

3
VOCABULARY PRACTICE   *Fill in the blank spaces, using the vocabulary words above. Choose words with meanings suggested by the words in parentheses.*

The (*shallow, underwater ledge near the shore*) _____ extends about 12 miles

out to sea. This part of the ocean was the first to be (*used by people for their own*

advantage) _____ by people. It is an ideal place for (*underwater agriculture*)

_____. We (*desire*) _____ the wealth of the ocean. We want to mine the

(*ocean floor*) _____. We also want to drill for (*some distance from the shore*)

_____ oil. When oil is drilled for, there is an occasional accident. A (*deadly*)

_____ amount of oil can seep into the water, killing the fish. This oil can

leave (*a sticky substance*) _____ on the beach. The (*great amount*) _____

of work in cleaning up the oil spill is (*unbelievable*) _____. Yet an oil spill is

but a (*commonplace*) _____ consequence of our hopes and dreams.

4 **VOCABULARY PRACTICE**   *Circle the answer (a, b, or c) most similar in meaning to the italicized word.*

1. For *millennia* people have exploited the land.
   a. decades
   b. thousands of years
   c. hundreds of years

2. Estimates of natural gas reserves have *tripled*.
   a. increased two times
   b. increased four times
   c. increased three times

3. There is a *scramble* for the ocean's reserves.
   a. competitive struggle
   b. regional plan
   c. new optimism

4. The most conservative estimates of the ocean's wealth *stagger* the imagination.
   a. to astound
   b. to walk unsteadily
   c. to frighten

5. Should the oceans be given to the strongest *pioneer*?
   a. last person to arrive
   b. first person to arrive
   c. most determined person

6. This wealth should be divided *equitably*.
   a. in equal parts
   b. fairly
   c. slowly

7. Some people underestimate the *lure* of the ocean's wealth.
   a. magnitude
   b. size
   c. attraction

8. The ocean might become a human *habitat*.
   a. place for swimming
   b. place for living
   c. place for fishing

9. Insecticides *seep* into the rivers.
   a. enter slowly
   b. enter rapidly
   c. enter in large quantities

10. Lethal chemicals can *contaminate* the water.
   a. improve
   b. spoil
   c. diminish

11. Fresh water can be *distilled* from sea water.
   a. obtained
   b. improved
   c. added

12. The continental shelf is under the *jurisdiction* of the federal government.
   a. sale
   b. loan
   c. authority

5
WORD-FORM CHART *Study the following words.*

PARTICIPLE	NOUN	VERB	ADJECTIVE	ADVERB
enriched enriching	riches	enrich	rich	richly
coveted coveting	covetousness	covet	covetous	covetously
dismissed dismissing	dismissal	dismiss		
dispersed dispersing	dispersion	disperse		
gladdened gladdening	gladness	gladden	glad	gladly
profited profiting	profit	profit	profitable	profitably
	potential		potential	potentially

PARTICIPLE	NOUN	VERB	ADJECTIVE	ADVERB
extracted extracting	extraction	extract		
	coast		coastal	
constricted constricting	constriction	constrict	constrictive	
gambled gambling	gamble gambler gambling	gamble		
restrained restraining	restraint	restrain		
lacked lacking	lack	lack		
authorized authorizing	authority	authorize	authoritative	authoritatively
	frivolity		frivolous	frivolously
disposed disposing	disposal	dispose		
economized economizing	economy	economize	economic	economically
exploited exploiting	exploitation exploiter	exploit		
conserved conserving	conservation	conserve	conservative	conservatively
speculated speculating	speculation	speculate	speculative	speculatively
contaminated contaminating	contaminating	contaminate		
isolated isolating	isolation	isolate		

6
WORD-FORM PRACTICE   *In the blank space, write the correct form of the italicized word.*

1. *frivolous*   June's parties are known for their fun and _____.

2. *gamble*   _____ is often expensive.

3. *authority*   The U.N. must act _____ on international problems.

4. *dispose*   _____ of the wealth from the sea is a world problem.

5. *disperse*   The _____ of insecticides in a river kills the fish.

6. *enrich*   People have destroyed the _____ of the land.

7. *dismissal*   The boss _____ several employees.

8. *glad*   She would _____ help her mother.

9. *lack*   The government _____ authority to act in that matter.

10. *restrain*   The courts show _____ in certain criminal cases.

11. *coastal*   Cities along the _____ may use the ocean for jet-age space.

12. *coast*   _____ cities attract tourists in the summer.

13. *economical* Our _____ has its ups and downs.

14. *potential*   The seabeds are _____ profitable.

15. *covet*   Our _____ could destroy the wealth of the oceans.

16. *authority*   Congress may _____ commercial use of the oceans.

17. *economy*   Industry must use the ocean's resources _____.

18. *rich*   The _____ of the ocean are still to be gathered.

19. *conserve*   According to _____ estimates, the world population will double by 2006.

20. *extract*   The _____ of minerals from the seabed involves complex technology.

7 *VERB PRACTICE   From the list below, select the verb that best completes the meaning of each sentence and insert it in the blank. Do not use any verb more than once.*

soaked	set off	drilled
estimated	revived	cultivated
distilled	disposed	reigned
divided	seeped	confused

1. Competition for the ocean's riches could _____ a new war.

2. Contaminants _____ slowly into our river systems.

3. The rain _____ the girl from head to foot.

4. The student fainted. Fresh air _____ her instantly.

5. Oil companies _____ for oil in the seabed.

6. Using a new process, the scientists _____ fresh water from salt water.

7. Not knowing the distance exactly, he _____ that it was five miles.

8. He _____ of the garbage by throwing it in the garbage can.

9. Using aquaculture, marine scientists _____ fish and plant life in the ocean.

10. The Queen ruled wisely. She _____ over England for many years.

8 *PARTICIPLES   In the blank space, insert the correct form of the participle. (Use the prefix un- in sentences 9 and 15.)*

1. *enrich*   _____ bread contains extra vitamins.

2. *enrich*   Travel is an _____ experience.

3. *contaminate*   Do not drink _____ water.

4. *authority*   Is this the _____ version of the Bible?

5. *isolate*   Robinson Crusoe was an _____ person on a desert island.

6. *constrict*   _____ arteries cause heart trouble.

7. *covet*   The athlete won the _____ prize.

8. *extract*   An _____ tooth can never cause trouble again.

9. *exploit*   Un_____ land is high in value.

10. *pollute*   _____ water is a poor habitat for fish.

11. *pollute*   Water-_____ chemicals are sometimes dumped in the ocean.

12. *contaminate*   Chemically _____ water must be cleaned up.

13. *contaminate*   Birds avoid _____ water.

14. *dismiss*   A _____ employee must find a new job.

15. *restrain*   Protest groups sometimes use un_____ violence.

9
READING COMPREHENSION I   *On the basis of the story, mark each of the following sentences T if it is true or F if it is false.*

1. ____ The oceans cover less than half the earth's surface.

2. ____ Four out of every five living things live in the oceans.

3. ____ There is little mineral wealth in the seabed.

4. ____ The oceans are an excellent place to dump atomic waste.

5. ____ Mining the ocean's minerals will never be practical.

6. ____ Manganese nodules are an important source of protein.

7. ____ Most of the ocean's minerals are found in shallow water.

8. ____ The U.S. gets less than 5 percent of its oil from offshore drilling.

9. ____ Aquaculture is a way of increasing farm production on land near the ocean.

10. ____ Present methods of fishing are at the "bow-and-arrow" level of technology.

11. ____ Offshore airports would reduce overcrowding in cities like New York and Los Angeles.

12. ____ Intense competition for the ocean's wealth will promote world peace.

13. ____ The world fish catch could be increased ten times if fish were cultivated like livestock.

14. ____ People may one day live in the oceans.

15. ____ In this article, the author expresses dissatisfaction with the present methods of settling international disputes over control and use of the oceans.

10 **READING COMPREHENSION II**   *Choose the wording (a, b, or c) that best completes each sentence. Then rewrite the sentence completely.*

1. The oceans cover nearly
   a. half the world.
   b. two-thirds of the world.
   c. three-quarters of the world.

2. People's competition for underwater riches could
   a. increase international tensions.
   b. improve international understanding.
   c. decrease international pollution.

3. Minerals are found in the ocean
   a. in limited supply.
   b. in lavish supply.
   c. infrequently.

4. The people who did not think we could mine the ocean are called
    a. optimists.
    b. pessimists.
    c. pioneers.

5. After an oil spill, the beaches are soaked in
    a. slime.
    b. seabed.
    c. protein.

6. Manganese nodules are
    a. a rare type of fish.
    b. small lumps of metal.
    c. offshore oil wells.

7. The reserves of manganese in the ocean are
    a. much larger than land reserves.
    b. about the same as land reserves.
    c. smaller than land reserves.

8. Most of the nodules are found in
    a. deep water.
    b. shallow water.
    c. near a reef.

9. In recent years, offshore production of oil
    a. has increased a lot.
    b. has decreased.
    c. has increased a little.

10. Aquaculture is a way of increasing our supply of
    a. fish and plant life.
    b. salt water.
    c. crude oil.

11. One reason for building an offshore city outside the country's territorial limit is
    a. to encourage gambling and avoid taxes.
    b. to get better water.
    c. to improve the seabed.

12. At the moment, legal questions about the oceans are
    a. easily settled by the U.N.
    b. easily settled by the Federal Government.
    c. very difficult to settle.

*11***CONTROLLED COMPOSITION**   *Rewrite the selection below. Follow the directions in each step.*

The Oceans

¹The oceans touch or surround most countries of the world. ²So fishing is an *industry* of international importance. ³Many fish are caught in the waters over the *shallow underseas ledge near the land*. ⁴To increase the catch, some countries are using *artificial cultivation of fish and plants*. ⁵But all this is spoiled when there is an oil *leak*. ⁶It can cover the water's surface with *sticky material* that is *deadly* to fish and birds.

⁷But fish are not the only resource. ⁸Minerals like manganese lie in small *lumps* on the *ocean floor*. ⁹One day the oceans might even become the *living place* for people themselves. ¹⁰The oceans are truly our last great resource.

1. Rewrite the passage, substituting synonyms from the reading for the italicized words.
2. When the compositions are finished, have students put their work on the blackboard.

*12***TOPICS FOR WRITING AND DISCUSSION**   *Before undertaking these topics, you may need to collect background information from an atlas or world map.*

1. How should the wealth of the oceans be divided? Here are some points to consider:
   A. Should each nation control the section of the ocean on its own borders? Thus Chile, with a long coastline, would control more water than Ecuador, while Switzerland, being landlocked, would have no ocean rights at all. Is this fair?
   B. How far from shore should the jurisdiction of each country extend? Some nations set a three-mile limit; others claim all the water within 200 miles of their coasts.
   C. Should each nation control both the fishing and mining rights, or the fishing rights only?
   D. Landlocked countries such as Hungary, Switzerland, Austria, Czechoslovakia, and Bolivia do not face an ocean. Should they be excluded from these benefits?
   E. Undeveloped nations may not possess the technology to develop the seabed. What should be done about this?

F. A way may soon be found to mine in deep water. How should the wealth in the *middle* of the ocean be divided?

G. Is it desirable for neighboring countries to join in regional planning for the best use of their share of the ocean's resources? Explain how to do this.

H. Who should settle legal questions about the ocean? Should it be the U.N., the World Court, or some other international body?

2. Most countries are threatened by air and water pollution, which has become an international problem. Tell how you would correct this situation.

3. What should your country do to develop the ocean's resources?

4. Describe a fishing or boating trip you have taken.

13 *DICTATION*

1. We covet the wealth of the oceans.
2. The oceans contain a lavish supply of minerals.
3. How can these resources be divided equally?
4. What is at stake?
5. Lethal chemicals contaminate the water.
6. Birds were soaked in oily slime.
7. The magnitude of the oceans is incredible.
8. Underwater farming is called aquaculture.
9. Can fresh water be distilled from sea water?
10. Who should control the continental shelf?

Appendix I

LANGUAGE GAMES

PICTURE GAME: "What Do You See?"

Divide the class into groups. For this game, use a photo in the text or a picture brought to class that contains a great mixture of people, objects, and activities. Have the class identify the main points of interest in the picture and write these words on the board. (The words can be erased midway through the game.)

The game begins with one team asking the other, "What do you see?" naming an area in the picture and the position of the object. For instance:

FIRST STUDENT: What do you see in the upper-left corner of the picture?
SECOND STUDENT: (asking for clarification) Where do you mean, exactly?
FIRST STUDENT: What do you see on the ceiling above the shelf?
SECOND STUDENT: I see lights.

Use directional words, such as *upper left, lower right, middle, center.* Use such relational words as *above, below, near, behind, in front of, next to, leaning toward, touching, not quite touching.* Use descriptive words, including *big, little, square, round, long, short, solid, rectangular, heavy, light.*

Do not accept single-word answers. All responses must be complete sentences.

Variation: Ask other kinds of questions. (1) "How many do you see?" (2) "What is the person in the middle of the picture doing?" (3) "In your opinion, why have the men (women) come to this place?" (4) "Using your imagination, tell me what you think the man did yesterday." (5) "What do you think the woman will do tomorrow?"

IDENTIFICATION GAME: *Clues and Questions*

This game is useful when a reading deals with topics that have identifying characteristics, such as foods (Chapter 2), musical instruments (Chapter 3), careers (Chapter 8), animals (Chapter 14). The purpose of the game is to ask questions that narrow the field until the object is identified.

Each team prepares a short list of items in the given category—foods, for instance. If necessary, some sample questions appropriate to this category can be suggested by the class and put on the board, as a warm-up. Then teams take turns, each member being allowed to ask one question of someone on the opposing team, who must respond in a complete sentence.

Example:

FIRST STUDENT: What color is the vegetable you're thinking of?
SECOND STUDENT: The vegetable I'm thinking of is white.
FIRST STUDENT: Does it grow in or above the ground?
SECOND STUDENT: It grows in the ground.

Wild guessing should be avoided in favor of getting the right answer through careful questioning. Each answer is worth one point. If a team guesses incorrectly, the other team tells the answer and no score is made.

SCRAMBLED SPELLING GAME

1. In the list below are ten familiar words from a reading, with two adjacent letters out of order. The object of the game is to unscramble the spelling and guess the word.

    Divide the class into groups. Each group must work together as a team, firing suggestions back and forth, until the right combination is found. The first team to unscramble the letters and spell all the words correctly wins the game. Here are some examples from Chapter I.

Example: C A Y N O N	Canyon
G E O L O Y G	Geology
1. D I N O S U A R S	_____
2. E R O S O I N	_____
3. S C E N R E Y	_____
4. C I L M A T E	_____

5. I N T R E U R B A N   _____
6. P R E C A M B R I N A   _____
7. V L O C A N O   _____
8. R E S T U A R A N T   _____
9. P R E C I P C I E   _____
10. P R E H I S O T R I C   _____

2. Next, have each team prepare its own list of ten scrambled words from the reading, with two letters out of order. Teams will exchange lists, and play will proceed as before, with group members working together. The first team to get all the words wins the game.

Suggestion: When teams become adept at this game, three or even four letters can be scrambled to increase the difficulty.

SPELLING GAME

Divide the class into groups. Have each group prepare a list of vocabulary words from those studied in the lesson. Taking turns, a group member will spell a word, omitting one letter. The player presenting the word will say, "space," when coming to the letter omitted, and then will call on someone in the opposing team to spell the word correctly. For example, if the word is "canyon," a student will say C – A – N – Y – space – N. Score should be kept. The team with the most points is the winner.

Game variations: (1) If students find it easy to spell words with one letter missing, omit two letters, or even three. (2) When the word has been spelled correctly, someone can be called on to use the word in a sentence, for an extra point.

Suggestion: Once the class understands the game, several teams can play simultaneously, each with a student monitor to referee the spelling and keep the score. The teacher can move around the room, providing any help that is needed.

WORD FAMILIES

In this game, students give a word and ask for a related form, or give a type of work and ask for the occupation, or a musical instrument and ask for the group, or an animal and ask for the type, and so on.

EXAMPLES

1. Word Form
   (any chapter)

   nutrition   (nutritious)

2. Musical Instruments
   (Chapter 3)

   violin   (stringed instrument)
   drum   (percussion instrument)

3. Occupations
   (Chapter 8)

   electricity   (electrician)
   law   (lawyer)
   plumbing   (plumber)

4. Animals
   (Chapter 14)

   bear   (carnivore or predator)
   robin   (bird)
   trout   (fish)

Appendix II

HOW TO USE A DICTIONARY

A good English dictionary is a storehouse of information and a necessity for a language student. To make a dictionary work for you, however, you must know how to use it. You must understand how the words are arranged and what to look for in the entries. You must also learn the meaning of the special symbols and abbreviations that enable the dictionary maker to concentrate a lot of information in a small space. Did you know that a little pocket-size dictionary has more than 57,000 entries, or that a larger, desk-size dictionary lists more than 100,000 words? To save space, much of this information must be put down in a special code. Study the pronunciation symbols and go through the other explanatory matter in your dictionary's preface. A little practice is required to learn what the abbreviations mean and how to use all the resources of the dictionary effectively. Go over the sample pages that follow, and work on the exercises. It would not be surprising if, henceforth, you find the dictionary your most valuable study aid, word builder, and reference tool.

EXERCISE I   *Use the sample pages for this exercise.*

1. Some words have several different definitions. You must select the meaning that best fits your sentence. For example, using the preceding pages from

—**SYN.** see TURN —**gy′ra′tor** *n.* —**gy′ra·to′ry** (-rə tôr′ē) *adj.*

gy·ra·tion (jī rā′shən) *n.* 1. the act of gyrating; circular or spiral motion 2. something gyrate, as a whorl

gyre (jīr) *n.* [L. *gyrus* < Gr. *gyros*, a circle: see GYRATE] [Chiefly Poet.] 1. a circular or spiral motion; whirl; revolution 2. a circular or spiral form; ring or vortex —*vi., vt.* **gyred, gyr′ing** [Chiefly Poet.] to whirl

☆**gy·rene** (jī rēn′) *n.* [< ?: cf. *Am. Speech*, Vol. XXXVII, No. 3, Oct., 1962] [Slang] a member of the U.S. Marine Corps

gyr·fal·con (jur′fal′kən, -fôl′-, -fô′-) *n.* [ME. *gerfaucoun* < OFr. *girfaucon* < Frank. *gerfalko* < *ger* (OHG. *gir*, hawk), lit., greedy (one) < IE. base *ĝhī, *ĝhe-, whence GAPE + *falko*, FALCON] a large, fierce, strong falcon (*Falco rusticolus*) of the arctic regions

gy·ro (jī′rō) *n., pl.* **-ros** 1. *short for* GYROSCOPE 2. *short for* GYROCOMPASS

gy·ro- (jī′rō, -rə) [′< Gr. *gyros*, a circle: see GYRATE] a *combining form meaning:* 1. gyrating [*gyroscope*] 2. gyroscope [*gyrocompass*] Also, before a vowel, **gyr-**

gy·ro·com·pass (-kum′pas) *n.* a compass consisting of a motor-operated gyroscope whose rotating axis, kept in a horizontal plane, takes a position parallel to the axis of the earth's rotation and thus points to the geographic north pole instead of to the magnetic pole

~~gyro horizon~~ *same* as ARTIFICIAL HORIZON (sense 1)

gy·ro·mag·net·ic (jī′rō mag net′ik) *adj.* of or pertaining to the magnetic properties of rotating charged particles

gy·ro·pi·lot (jī′rō pī′lət) *n. same as* AUTOMATIC PILOT

gy·ro·plane (jī′rə plän′) *n.* [GYRO- + PLANE²] any aircraft having wings that rotate about a vertical or nearly vertical axis, as the autogiro or helicopter

(margin note: centered period for syllable division)

gy·ro·scope (-skōp′) *n.* [GYRO- + -SCOPE] a wheel mounted in a ring so that its axis is free to turn in any direction: when the wheel is spun rapidly, it will keep its original plane of rotation no matter which way the ring is turned: gyroscopes are used in gyrocompasses and to keep moving ships, airplanes, etc. level —**gy′ro·scop′ic** (-skäp′ik) *adj.* —**gy′ro·scop′i·cal·ly** *adv.*

gy·rose (jī′rōs) *adj.* [< GYRE + -OSE²] *Bot.* marked with wavy lines or convolutions

gy·ro·sta·bi·liz·er (jī′rō stā′bə lī′zər) *n.* a device consisting of a gyroscope spinning in a vertical plane, used to stabilize the side-to-side rolling of a ship

GYROSCOPE

gy·ro·stat (jī′rə stat′) *n.* [GYRO- + -STAT] a gyroscope consisting of a rotating wheel set in a case, used for demonstrating the dynamics of rotating bodies

gy·ro·stat·ic (jī′rə stat′ik) *adj.* 1. of a gyrostat 2. of gyrostatics

gy·ro·stat·ics (-iks) *n.pl. [with sing. v.]* [GYRO- + STATICS] the branch of physics dealing with rotating bodies and their tendency to maintain their plane of rotation

gy·rus (jī′rəs) *n., pl.* **-ri** (-rī) [ModL. < L.: see GYRE] *Anat.* a convoluted ridge or fold between fissures, or sulci, esp. of the cortex of the brain

gyve (jīv) *n., vt.* **gyved, gyv′ing** [ME. *give* < Anglo-Fr. *gyves*, pl. < ? ME. *withe*, thong, band: cf. WITHY] [Archaic or Poet.] fetter; shackle

H

(label: part of speech label)

(label: plural)

H, h (āch) *n., pl.* **H's, h's** 1. the eighth letter of the English alphabet: from the Greek *eta*, a borrowing from the Phoenician 2. the sound of *H* or *h*, phonetically a rough breathing (aspirate): a glottal fricative in which the glottis gradually narrows toward the position for voicing the following vowel while the tongue and lips assume the position for articulating it; in many words originally from French, as *honor, honest*, initial *h* is silent 3. a type or impression for *H* or *h* 4. *a symbol for* the eighth in a sequence or group —*adj.* 1. of *H* or *h* 2. eighth in a sequence or group

H (āch) *n.* 1. an object shaped like *H* 2. *Chem. the symbol for* hydrogen 3. *Physics the symbol for: a)* henry *b)* the horizontal component of terrestrial magnetism 4. [Slang] heroin —*adj.* shaped like *H*

H., h. 1. harbor 2. hard 3. hardness 4. height 5. high 6. *Baseball* hits 7. hour(s) 8. hundred 9. husband

ha (hä) *interj.* [echoic] an exclamation variously expressing wonder, surprise, anger, triumph, etc.: repeated (**ha-ha**) it may indicate laughter, derision, etc. —*n.* the sound of this exclamation or of a laugh

ha. hectare(s)

h.a. [L. *hoc anno*] in this year

(margin note: abbreviation)

Haa·kon VII (hô′koon) 1872–1957; king of Norway (1905–57)

Haar·lem (här′ləm) city in NW Netherlands; capital of North Holland province: pop. 172,000

Haar·lem·mer·meer (här′lə mər mer′) city in NW Netherlands, on the site of a former lake: pop. 51,000

Ha·bak·kuk (hab′ə kuk, hə bak′ək) [Heb. *habhaqqūq*, prob. < *hābaq*, to embrace] *Bible* 1. a Hebrew prophet of about the 7th century B.C. 2. the book containing his prophecies: abbrev. **Hab.** Also, in the Douay Bible, **Ha′ba·cuc**

Ha·ba·na (ä bä′ nä), (La) *Sp. name of* HAVANA

ha·ba·ne·ra (hä′bə ner′ə; *Sp.* ä′bä nä′rä) *n.* [Sp., lit., of HABANA] 1. a slow Cuban dance similar to the tango 2. the music for this

ha·be·as cor·pus (hā′bē əs kôr′pəs) [ME. < L., (that) you have the body] *Law* any of various writs ordering a person to be brought before a court; specif., a writ or order requiring that a detained person be brought before a court at a stated time and place to decide the legality of his detention or imprisonment: in full, **habeas corpus ad sub·ji·ci·en·dum** (ad′ səb yik′ē en′dəm): the right of *habeas corpus* safeguards one against illegal detention or imprisonment

(margin note: capitalized)

(margin note: foreign word)

Ha·ber (hä′bər), **Fritz** 1868–1934; Ger. chemist

hab·er·dash·er (hab′ər dash′ər, hab′ə-) *n.* [ME. *haberdashere*, prob. < Anglo-Fr. *hapertas*, kind of cloth] 1. a person whose work or business is selling men's furnishings,

such as hats, shirts, neckties, gloves, etc. 2. [Brit.] a dealer in various small articles, such as ribbons, thread, needles, etc.

hab·er·dash·er·y (-ē) *n., pl.* **-er·ies** [ME. *haberdasshrie*] 1. things sold by a haberdasher 2. a haberdasher's shop

hab·er·geon (hab′ər jən) *n.* [ME. *habergoun* < OFr. *haubergeon*, dim. of *hauberc*: see HAUBERK] 1. a short, high-necked jacket of mail, usually sleeveless 2. *same as* HAUBERK

hab·ile (hab′il) *adj.* [ME. *habil* < OFr. *habile* < L. *habilis* < base of *habere*: see HABIT] [Now Rare] able; skillful; handy; clever

ha·bil·i·ment (hə bil′ə mənt) *n.* [MFr. *habillement* < *habiller*, to clothe, make fit < *habile*: see prec.] 1. [*usually pl.*] clothing; dress; attire 2. [*pl.*] furnishings or equipment; trappings

ha·bil·i·tate (-tāt′) *vt.* **-tat′ed, -tat′ing** [< ML. *habilitatus*, pp. of *habilitare*, to make suitable < L. *habilis* (see HABILE)] 1. to clothe; equip; outfit 2. to educate or train (the mentally or physically handicapped, the disadvantaged, etc.) to function better in society 3. *Mining* to provide (a mine) with the capital and equipment needed to work (it) —**ha·bil′i·ta′tion** *n.* —**ha·bil′i·ta′tive** *adj.*

hab·it (hab′it) *n.* [ME. < OFr. < L. *habitus*, condition, appearance, dress < pp. of *habere*, to have, hold < IE. base *ghabh-*, to grasp, take, whence GIVE] 1. formerly, costume; dress 2. a particular costume showing rank, status, etc.; specif., *a)* a distinctive religious costume [a monk's *habit*] *b)* a costume worn for certain occasions [a riding *habit*] 3. habitual or characteristic condition of mind or body; disposition 4. *a)* a thing done often and hence, usually, done easily; practice; custom *b)* a pattern of action that is acquired and has become so automatic that it is difficult to break 5. a tendency to perform a certain action or behave in a certain way; usual way of doing 6. an addiction, esp. to narcotics 7. *Biol.* the tendency of a plant or animal to grow in a certain way; characteristic growth [a twining *habit*] —*vt.* 1. to dress; clothe 2. [Archaic] to inhabit

SYN.—**habit** refers to an act repeated so often by an individual that it has become automatic with him [his *habit* of tugging at his ear in perplexity]; **practice** also implies the regular repetition of an act but does not suggest that it is automatic [the *practice* of reading in bed]; **custom** applies to any act or procedure carried on by tradition and often enforced by social disapproval of any violation [the *custom* of dressing for dinner]; **usage** refers to custom or practice that has become sanctioned through being long established [*usage* is the only authority in language]; **wont** is a literary or somewhat archaic equivalent for **practice** [it was his *wont* to rise early]

(label: synonym)

hab·it·a·ble (-ə b'l) *adj.* [ME. < OFr. < L. *habitabilis* < *habitare*, to have possession of, inhabit: see prec. & -ABLE] that can be inhabited; fit to be lived in —**hab'it·a·bil'i·ty** *n.* —**hab'it·a·bly** *adv.*

hab·it·ant (-ənt) *n.* [Fr. < L. *habitans*, prp.: see HABITABLE] 1. an inhabitant; resident 2. (*also Fr.* à bē tän') a farmer in Louisiana or Canada of French descent: also **hab·i·tan** (å bē tän')

hab·i·tat (hab'ə tat') *n.* [L., it inhabits: see HABITABLE] 1. the region where a plant or animal naturally grows or lives; native environment 2. the place where a person or thing is ordinarily found

hab·i·ta·tion (hab'ə tā'shən) *n.* [ME. *habitacioun* < OFr. *habitacion* < L. *habitatio*: see HABITABLE] 1. the act of inhabiting; occupancy 2. a place in which to live; dwelling; home 3. a colony or settlement

hab·it-form·ing (hab'it fôr'miŋ) *adj.* resulting in the formation of a habit or in addiction

ha·bit·u·al (hə bich'ōō wəl) *adj.* [ML. *habitualis*, of habit or dress: see HABIT] 1. formed or acquired by continual use; done by habit or fixed as a habit; customary 2. being or doing a certain thing by habit; steady; inveterate [a *habitual* smoker] 3. much seen, done, or used; usual; frequent —*SYN.* see USUAL — **ha·bit'u·al·ly** *adv.* —**ha·bit'u·al·ness** *n.*

ha·bit·u·ate (-ōō wāt') *vt.* -at'ed, -at'ing [< LL. *habituatus*, pp. of *habituare*, to bring into a condition or habit of the body < L. *habitus*: see HABIT] 1. to make used (*to*); accustom; familiarize: often used reflexively 2. [Archaic] to attend or visit often; frequent —**ha·bit'u·a'tion** *n.*

hab·i·tude (hab'ə tōōd', -tyōōd') *n.* [ME. *abitude* < MFr. *habitude* < L. *habitudo*, condition, habit: see HABIT] 1. habitual or characteristic condition of mind or body; disposition 2. usual way of doing something; custom

ha·bit·u·é (hə bich'ōō wā') *n.* [Fr. < pp. of *habituer*, to accustom < LL. *habituare*: see HABITUATE] a person who frequents a certain place or places [a *habitué* of nightclubs]

hab·i·tus (hab'ə təs) *n., pl.* **hab'i·tus** (-tōōs) [ModL. < L., HABIT] 1. *same as* HABIT (*n.* 5, 7) 2. general physical appearance and body build, sometimes related to a predisposition to certain diseases

Habs·burg (häps'bōōrkh) *same as* HAPSBURG

ha·chure (hə shoor'; *also, for n.,* hash'oor) *n.* [Fr. < OFr. *hacher*, to chop < *hache*, ax < Frank. *hapja*, sickle < IE. base *(s)kep-*, whence SHAFT & L. *capo*, capon, Gr. *koptein*, to chop] any of a series of short parallel lines used, esp. in map making, to represent a sloping or elevated surface —*vt.* -**chured'**, -**chur'ing** to show by, or shade with, hachures

☆**ha·ci·en·da** (hä'sē en'də, has'ē-) *n.* [Sp. < OSp. *facienda*, employment, estate < L. *facienda*, things to be done < *facere*: see FACT] in Spanish America, 1. a large estate, ranch, or plantation 2. the main dwelling on any of these

Ha·ci·en·da Heights (hä'sē en'də, has'ē-) suburb of Los Angeles, in SW Calif.: pop. 36,000

hack¹ (hak) *vt.* [ME. *hacken* < OE. *haccian*, akin to G. *hacken* < IE. base **keg-*, peg, hook, whence HOOK, HATCHEL] 1. *a)* to chop or cut crudely, roughly, or irregularly, as with a hatchet *b)* to shape, trim, damage, etc. with or as with rough, sweeping strokes 2. to break up (land) with a hoe, mattock, etc. ☆3. *Basketball* to foul by striking the arm of (an opponent who has the ball) with the hand or arm 4. *Rugby* to foul by kicking (an opponent) on the shins —*vi.* 1. to make rough or irregular cuts 2. to give harsh, dry coughs ☆3. *Basketball* to hack an opponent —*n.* 1. a tool for cutting or hacking; ax, hoe, mattock, etc. 2. a slash, gash, or notch made by a sharp implement 3. a hacking blow 4. a harsh, dry cough —☆**hack around** [Colloq.] to engage in aimless activity; spend time idly —**hack'er** *n.*

hack² (hak) *n.* [contr. < HACKNEY] 1. *a)* a horse for hire *b)* a horse for all sorts of work *c)* a saddle horse *d)* an old, worn-out horse 2. a person hired to do routine, often dull, writing; literary drudge ☆3. a worker for a political party, usually holding office through patronage, who serves his leaders devotedly and unquestioningly 4. a carriage or coach for hire 5. [Colloq.] *a)* a taxicab *b)* a hackman or cabdriver —*vt.* 1. to employ as a hack 2. to hire out (a horse, etc.) 3. to wear out or make stale by constant use —*vi.* 1. [Brit.] to jog along on a horse ☆2. [Colloq.] to drive a taxicab —*adj.* 1. employed as a hack [a *hack* writer] 2. done by a hack [*hack* work] 3. stale; trite; hackneyed

hack³ (hak) *n.* [orig., based on which a falcon's meat was put, var. of HATCH²] 1. a grating or rack for drying cheese or fish, holding food for cattle, etc. 2. a pile or row of unburned bricks set out to dry —*vt.* to place on a hack for drying

☆**hack·a·more** (hak'ə môr') *n.* [altered < Sp. *jaquima*, halter < Ar. *shakima*] [Western] a rope or rawhide halter with a headstall, used in breaking horses

hack·ber·ry (hak'ber'ē) *n., pl.* -**ries** [< Scand., as in Dan. *hæggebær*, Norw. *haggebär*, ON. *heggr*: for IE. base see HEDGE] ☆1. any of a genus (*Celtis*) of American trees of the elm family, with a small fruit resembling a cherry ☆2. its fruit or its wood

hack·but (hak'but') *n.* [Fr. *haquebut* < obs. Du. *hakebus* < *hake*, *haak*, HOOK + *bus*, a gun, gun barrel, lit., box: so named from method of support during firing] an obsolete type of portable firearm; kind of harquebus

Hack·en·sack (hak'n sak') [< Du. < AmInd. (Delaware) name] city in NE N.J.: pop. 36,000

hack hammer a tool like an adz with a hammerhead, used in dressing stone

☆**hack·ie** (hak'ē) *n.* [Colloq.] a taxicab driver

hack·le¹ (hak''l) *n.* [ME. *hechele* (akin to G. *hechel*) < OE. **hæcel* < IE. base **keg-*, a peg, hook, whence HACK¹, HOOK: senses 2, 3, & 4, prob. infl. by dial. *hackle*, bird's plumage, animal's skin < OE. *hacele*] 1. a comblike instrument for separating the fibers of flax, hemp, etc. 2. *a)* any of the long, slender feathers at the neck of a rooster, peacock, pigeon, etc. *b)* such feathers, collectively 3. *Fishing a)* a tuft of feathers from a rooster's neck, used in making artificial flies *b)* a fly made with a hackle 4. [*pl.*] the hairs on a dog's neck and back that bristle, as when the dog is ready to fight —*vt.* -**led**, -**ling** 1. to separate the fibers of (flax, hemp, etc.) with a hackle 2. [Rare] to supply (a fishing fly) with a hackle —**get one's hackles up** to become tense with anger; bristle

hack·le² (hak''l) *vt., vi.* -**led**, -**ling** [freq. of HACK¹] to cut roughly; mangle

☆**hack·man** (hak'mən) *n., pl.* -**men** (-mən) the driver of a hack or carriage for hire

☆**hack·ma·tack** (hak'mə tak') *n.* [AmInd. (Algonquian)] 1. *same as* TAMARACK 2. the balsam poplar (*Populus balsamifera*) or the willow family 3. the wood of either of these trees

hack·ney (hak'nē) *n., pl.* -**neys** [ME. *hakene, hakenei* < *Hakeney* (now *Hackney*), an English village] 1. a horse for ordinary driving or riding 2. a carriage for hire 3. [Obs.] a person hired for dull, monotonous work; drudge —*adj.* [Obs.] 1. hired out 2. trite; commonplace —*vt.* [Now Rare] 1. to hire out 2. to make trite by overuse

hack·neyed (-nēd') *adj.* made trite and commonplace by overuse —*SYN.* see TRITE

hack·saw (hak'sô') *n.* a saw for cutting metal, consisting of a narrow, fine-toothed blade held in a frame: also **hack saw**

had (had; *unstressed* həd, əd) [ME. *hadde, had* < OE. *hæfde*] *pt. & pp.* of HAVE: also used to indicate preference or necessity, with adverbs, adjectives, and phrases of comparison, such as *rather, better, as well* (Ex.: I had better leave)

HACKSAW

had·dock (had'ək) *n., pl.* -**dock**, -**docks**: see PLURAL, II, D, 2 [ME *hadok* < ? OFr. *hadot*, kind of salt fish] a food fish (*Melanogrammus aeglefinus*) related to the cod, found off the coasts of Europe and N. America

hade (hād) *n.* [< dial. *hade*, to slope, incline < ?] *Geol.* the angle between the plane of a fault or vein and the vertical plane —*vi.* **had'ed, had'ing** *Geol.* to incline from the vertical plane, as a fault, vein, or lode

Ha·des (hā'dēz) [Gr. *Haidēs*] 1. *Gr. Myth. a)* the home of the dead, beneath the earth *b)* the ruler of the underworld 2. *Bible* the state or resting place of the dead: name used in some modern translations of the New Testament —*n.* [*often* h-] [Colloq.] hell: a euphemism

Ha·dhra·maut, Ha·dra·maut (hä'drä môt') 1. region on the S coast of Arabia, in E Southern Yemen: c. 58,500 sq. mi. 2. river valley (**Wadi Hadhramaut**) that crosses this region: c. 350 mi.

hadj (haj) *n. same as* HAJJ

hadj·i (-ē) *n. same as* HAJJI

had·n't (had''nt) had not

Ha·dri·an (hā'drē ən) (L. name *Publius Aelius Hadrianus*) 76–138 A.D.; Roman emperor (117–138)

Hadrian's Wall stone wall across N England, from Solway Firth to the Tyne: built (122–128 A.D.) by Hadrian to protect Roman Britain from N tribes: 73 1/2 mi.

hadst (hadst) *archaic 2d pers. sing., past indic.,* of HAVE: *used with* thou

hae (hā, ha) *vt.* [Scot.] to have

Haeck·el (hek'əl), **Ernst Hein·rich** (ernst hīn'riH) 1834–1919; Ger. biologist & philosopher

haem-, haema-, haemat-, haemato-, haemo- *same as* HEM-, HEMA-, HEMAT-, HEMATO-, HEMO-

hae·ma·tox·y·lon (hē'mə täk'sə län', hem'ə-) *n.* [ModL. *haematoxylon* < HAEMATO- + Gr. *xylon*, wood] *same as* LOGWOOD: see also HEMATOXYLIN

-hae·mi·a (hē'mē ə) *same as* -EMIA

hae·res (hē'rēz) *n., pl.* **hae·re·des** (hə rē'dēz) *same as* HERES

Ha·fiz (hä fiz') (born *Shams-ud-Din Mohammed*) 14th cent.; Per. lyric poet

ha·fiz (häf'iz) *n.* [Ar. *hāfiz*, a person who remembers] *title* for a Moslem who has memorized the Koran

haf·ni·um (haf'nē əm) *n.* [ModL. < L. *Hafnia*, Roman name of Copenhagen] a metallic chemical element found with zirconium and somewhat resembling it: used in the manufacture of tungsten filaments and in reactor control

the dictionary, find the best definition for each of the italicized words below. Write the definition on the line.

   A. I always eat supper at 6:30 P.M. It is my *habit.*

         _____

   B. A soldier usually dresses in a military *habit.*

         _____

   C. Joe does uninteresting *hack* work in an office.

         _____

   D. In the 19th century, a common form of transportation was the horse-drawn *hack.*

         _____

2. What is the adjective form of *habit?* (Find the noun *habit* and then look around for the adjective form of this word. It will be labeled *adj.*)

_____

3. A *haberdashery* is a men's clothing shop. What is a person called who works in or operates such a store?

_____

4. A *haddock* is a kind of saltwater fish. What other fish is related to it and in

what waters is the haddock found? _____

5. From what language does English borrow each of the following words?

original language   *meaning*

hacienda _____ _____

Hades _____ _____

habanera _____ _____

6. Explain the difference between *habitat* and *habitation.*

_____

7. In which country do you find *Hadrian's Wall?*

_____

8. What part of speech is each of the following words?

part of speech

habituate _____

hacksaw _____

gyrose _____

9. What is the derivation of the term *habeas corpus*?

_____

10. List two synonyms for *habit*.

_____

_____

EXERCISE II   *Using your dictionary, answer the following questions.*

1. Several meanings are given for each of the following italicized words. Find the definition that fits each sentence. Write the best definition on the line.

   A. Marilyn Monroe was a movie *star*. She has been in several films.

   _____

   B. The sun is our closest *star*.

   _____

   C. The *climate* in my country is always nice.

   _____

   D. The *climate* of opinion was unfavorable.

   _____

2. The following words are called "compounds." Some are written as one word, some as a hyphenated word, and some as two words. Check each pair in your dictionary and write the correct form in the blank space.

   A. down stairs (*adv.*) _____

   B. house fly (*n.*) _____

    C. free standing (*adj.*) _____

    D. free university (*n.*) _____

    E. half truth (*n.*) _____

    F. fair trade (*adj.*) _____

3. *Drop out* is a two-word verb. What does it mean?

_____

4. What is the adjective form of *caution?*

_____

5. What part of speech is *blowup?*

_____

EXERCISE III   *Use your dictionary to answer the following questions.*

1. *Lb.* is an abbreviation. What does it mean?

_____

2. What kind of work does a *redcap* do?

_____

3. Two American organizations frequently in the news are the *FBI* and the *CIA.* Write out in full the meanings of these abbreviations.

_____

4. *Manila hemp* is used to make rope. In what country did this name originate?

_____

5. Is a *loan shark* a kind of fish? Explain.

_____

Appendix III

HANDWRITING PRACTICE

This is an optional, self-help section for students who need to improve their penmanship.

It is no advantage in life to have handwriting that is difficult to read. On the contrary, neat, legible writing will help you at school and work. Even in today's world of the electric typewriter and word processor, good writing is still a very useful skill.

I. Analysis. *In your usual writing style, copy the model sentence on the blank line below. Then compare the two versions. Are your letters clear, uniform, open and well shaped, evenly spaced, the same height, slanted alike? If not, do the practice exercises. You will be surprised by how quickly your writing improves.*

Model: *The girl in the bright green dress raised her hand.*

Your writing:—————————————————————————

II A. Small Letters. *These 13 letters take half a line:* a, c, l, i,

m, n, o, r, s, u, v, w, x. *On composition paper, copy the model letters. Practice each letter by itself.*

a a a a   n n n   v v v

c c c c   o o o o   w w w

l l l l   r r r   x x x

i i i i i   s s s

m m m   u u u

II B. *These 6 letters are almost a whole line tall:* b, d, h, k, l, t

Practice each letter separately.

b b b b b   k k k k

d d d d   l l l l l

h h h h   t t t t t

II C. *These 7 letters drop below the line:* f, g, j, p, q, y, z

Practice each letter separately.

f f f f f   q q q q

g g g g   y y y

j j j j   z z z

p p p p

III Word Practice. *Copy these words on your composition paper. Make your letters the same size, evenly spaced, slanted alike. Practice each word separately.*

ice ice ice   judge judge   hot hot

do do do   jingle jingle   cute cute

can can can   discovered   alert alert

man man   beside beside   zoo zoo

rove rove   vixen vixen   zero zero

IV Capital Letters. *Practice copying these letters on your paper:*

A A A   G G G   M M   S S S   Y Y

B B B B   H H H   N N   T T   Z Z

C C C C   I I I I   O O   U U

D D D   J J J   P P   V V

E E E   K K K   Q Q   W W

F F F   L L L   R R   X X

V Sentences. *Copy these sentences on your paper. Review the small letters and the capitals. Be critical of your work. Continue to practice letters that are poorly shaped, uneven, off the line.*

The car hit the cat.
The lion lives in the zoo.
Many countries face the ocean.
He found the treasure. It was buried in the sand. They divided the gold.

ACKNOWLEDGMENTS

PHOTO CREDITS

page 2	Robert Lugton
page 3	Greyhound Bus Company
page 4	Department of Interior, Grand Canyon National Park
page 5	Neg. No. 335199 (Photo: R. E. Logan). Courtesy Department of Library Services, American Museum of Natural History.
page 21	Courtesy U.S. Department of Agriculture
page 22	Courtesy of Grand Union
page 23	Owen Franken, Stock, Boston
page 40	The Bettman Archive, Inc., 136 E. 57th St., New York, N.Y. 10022
page 42	Stan Wakefield
page 56	The Bettmann Archive, Inc., 136 E. 57th St., New York, N.Y. 10022
page 70	Teri Leigh Stratford
page 71	Tery Leigh Stratford
page 72	Ken Karp
page 83	Teri Leigh Stratford
page 84	Teri Leigh Stratford
page 85	Bill Fitz-Patrick, The White House
page 96	Ken Karp
page 97	(Top) Ken Karp (Bottom) Teri Leigh Stratford
page 107	Laimute E. Durskis
page 108	Laimute E. Durskis
page 111	Fernando Bujunes
page 113	NASA
page 115	(Left) Ken Karp (right) J. Mohr
page 127	Fleetwood Enterprises
page 128	Teri Leigh Stratford

page 129	(Top) Arthur Lavine
	(Bottom) Interbank Card Association
page 161	Denny Curtain
page 162	S. R. Flourney, U.S. Department of Agriculture Soil Conservation Service
page 180	Courtesy of the American Museum of Natural History
page 182	Culver Pictures, Inc., N.Y.
page 183	Monkmeyer Press Photo Service
page 200	Hella Hammid
page 201	(Top) Ken Karp
	(Bottom) Charles Gatewood
page 203	Ken Karp
page 204	Ken Karp
page 216	Colorado Game and Fish, U.S. Fish and Wildlife Service
page 218	Greenpeace
page 234	J. Frank, United Nations
page 236	D. Clarke, United Nations

TEXT CREDITS

"The Story of Jazz" and "Taking Stock of Your Family Finances" were co-authored by Albert L. Weeks, New York University.

"Can This Marriage Be Saved?" adapted from Dorothy Cameron Disney, "My Husband Has the No-Job Blues," *Ladies' Home Journal,* February 1983. Reprinted by permission of Ladies' Home Journal. Copyright 1983 by Downe Publishing, Inc.

"Ski Touring: A Fast-Growing Sport" adapted from William A. Davis, "Ski Touring," *The American Way,* January 1974. Reprinted in adapted form by permission of the author and *The American Way.*

"Our Disappearing Wildlife" adapted from Lisa J. Shawver, "North American Wildlife: The Vanishing Act," *Science News,* June 1974. Reprinted with permission from *Science News,* the weekly news magazine of science and the applications of science. Copyright 1974 by Science Service, Inc.

"The Oceans: Man's Last Great Resource" adapted from Claiborne Pell, *Saturday Review,* October 1969. Reprinted by permission of the author and the publisher.